The Inexhaustible Always in the Exhausted Speaks

The Inexhaustible Always in the Exhausted Speaks

A Sensorium of Brokenness and Delight

DOUGLAS B. OLDS

RESOURCE *Publications* · Eugene, Oregon

THE INEXHAUSTIBLE ALWAYS IN THE EXHAUSTED SPEAKS
A Sensorium of Brokenness and Delight

Copyright © 2025 Douglas B. Olds. All rights reserved. Except for brief quotations in critical publications or reviews, no part of this book may be reproduced in any manner without prior written permission from the publisher. Write: Permissions, Wipf and Stock Publishers, 199 W. 8th Ave., Suite 3, Eugene, OR 97401.

Resource Publications
An Imprint of Wipf and Stock Publishers
199 W. 8th Ave., Suite 3
Eugene, OR 97401

www.wipfandstock.com

PAPERBACK ISBN: 979-8-3852-5418-7
HARDCOVER ISBN: 979-8-3852-5419-4
EBOOK ISBN: 979-8-3852-5420-0
VERSION NUMBER 07/30/25

τελείων δέ ἐστιν ἡ στερεὰ τροφή, τῶν διὰ τὴν ἕξιν τὰ αἰσθητήρια γεγυμνασμένα ἐχόντων πρὸς διάκρισιν καλοῦ τε καὶ κακοῦ[1]

---

1. Heb 5:14. Author's exegetical paraphrase: "[In terms of v. 13's *word of righteousness*,] solid food is for the perfecting—those whose sensory faculties of awareness have, through ethical proficiency, been completely trained for the purpose of distinguishing good and evil—the spiritually re-constructive and ruinous—in the world."

Contents

To interrogate every claim | 1

I. Partuition: Germinate, Orient, Descend, Wither, Recrawl

Like Moses | 5
Acorns | 6
Shema | 9
Stranded mid-swell without biscuit | 11
Grief's Passing | 12
Billet to Savor | 14
Freedom's Credo (Mark 2:21) | 16
Apophatic this draw array, | 17
Fountain of Blessing | 18
Pathing a Doubling Blaze | 20

II. Landfall: Songs Discovering Ruptured Earth

Muse(um) [May 13, 2024] | 23
The Bell Epoc | 25
Listerlescene™ abandoned | 27
Derivatives | 29
Virtued Def/viance | 32
Entelechy (Valentine's Day 2023) | 34
This Is a Land Where Tears Gush | 35
I Dancing into We | 37
You, Me, and the Rocking Sea | 39
Hold, Partner, for the Dip | 40
Noticing Things | 41

III. Sailing: Ten Crossings through Wind and Word

Rushing Child and Taming Breeze | 45
A Michigan to My Lips (1958-) | 47
Haiku Sequence | 50
A Bullet's Durruti | 52
After Machined Confession, Ecclesiastes 7:10 | 54
This Bark Manacling | 56
Invitation to the Dance | 57
The Postmortem of Poetry | 58
In Need Jars Memory, My Churning | 61
Shape-Shifting Tissue, His Scheme | 62

IV. Mirrored: Human Refractions by Theory

Today's dating advice | 65
Drago(o)n's Feast | 67
As I Now Virgil Guide | 68
crucible of repair | 70
medicina animae—patristic logic | 72
Codex Carmina Viri-tudinex | 75
A bird may talon the sky | 76
Bird Feeder Fable | 78
Let the Dead Bury the Dead | 80
Fissured Runways | 82
Hibernetic Dispatch | 83
Those Boots (102323) | 87

V. BC (1980s canēns): Canon of Becoming in Bone and Blood Ascending

A Dive (that Cometh) | 91
None doubt some mantid trick of measled night | 92
Ontogeny | 93
Cladogram | 95
A Brief Metaphysics of Memory | 97
High-Speed Phylogeny | 99
(superconductivity) | 101
Semi-Conductivity | 103
Short Bahama | 104
Palm Sunday, 1989 | 107

Manta a-whorl by the fleeing burn | 109
Seen of Burma | 111
Potomac Segment | 113
transpire | 114
Boleti | 116
Dalmanutha | 117
Mind's autumn | 119
Requiem fragment | 120
February's Linted Solace | 122

VI. Pillows Tossed: Arcs of Parting through Wounded Grace

Does historical logic— | 125
Image the man— | 127
Birth of Tragedy | 129
Vacations from Wrathtown | 131
Scoffers | 133
Routed to Logroño (July 2023) | 135
Entering traffic hot | 138
Freed by the poppy's embracing wind! | 139
Peripetetic Accounts | 142
Genius | 145
Thursday Before Christmas, 2023 | 146
Upon Loosing a Tooth (A First Poem for 2024) | 147
Calling Water | 148
What war is this without foe? | 149
Dooring the Course of Youth | 150
Arms' Thorn Intending Embrace | 153
F(l)orward From Froward | 154
Ex Gloria Homeostasi | 160
Moon and Stars Clouded Released | 161
Bobcat's Aurora (May 11, 2024) | 162
To Fiber Galaxies | 163
Analogia Entrance | 164

VII. Back Down Modern: When by tent or text leads the Sun

Orbituaries | 169
As the Deer | 170
Umbrellas | 172
Back it Up | 173

Outposted Modern | 174
Fatherhood | 176
American Pastoral | 177
Recollection | 178
Election Day Eve Abstraction 2024 | 179

VIII. Unbunkering

The Roustings | 183
The Risk of Falling | 185
Evangelism | 187
Muddy channel runoff into bay (12242024) | 189
Calendars' Midnight Eliding | 190
Light Which a Silence Learns Her Craft | 192
Ship of State, Ship of Fools | 194
Tree of Life | 195
Moonshone Earth (01122025) | 197
Millworking Adumbration | 199
Shepherd's Pipe | 202
Blessed to escape | 206

IX. Tracking Energies' After Imaging

Anthroprologos | 211
Gracescape/ing | 212
Anatomy's Unbuckling | 214
Virgins' Heaven Rejoice | 217
Aura Abouting 12262024 | 219
Imagine Surveying like Goethe | 220
Psalm 2:2–3 and the Deep(ening) State | 223
San Francisco, September 9, 2020 | 224
Last Monday | 226
A Whispered *Credo* | 227
Listens the Helm, Writes the Rudder | 230

X. Wending from Lethe to the Styx:
Judgment kindles when Sensorial Denouement is attempted

Of Compacting the Present for Its Trash Ores | 235
Speciolatry | 241
Hiding Eggs Theater | 244
The Armchair Beckons (Psalm 7:15) | 250

Attendings | 252
Wounds are a signal of the vanity of violence (John 20:27) | 255
Christ's suborning esoteric— | 258
The East hills emerge | 260
A Great Lakes' Theodicy | 261
Heaven's Seventh, Walking | 263
Anendophasiac | 264
Under Second Heaven: A Theodicy of Arrest | 266
Sandtrapped by the Mars Invitational | 268
Ludd's Last Stand | 272
A-Nulling (A Coda) | 277
Postludic | 279

Fragments and Foundlings | 281

Afterward (Postlude as Prologue) | 284

So up from streetsetting glossolalia | 290

TO INTERROGATE EVERY CLAIM

of absolute and transcendence,
milling the lumbrous and prodding the slumberous,
turning their milieux, metaphor by metaphor,
lathed and reglazing
into the plank energies civil.

Moving,
from human nature

snared by ego's self-recursive wincing
and history trapped in repetition,
typecast by pessimists,

for the human essence—
joining together in the here and now's conative grace,
ever by virtues vesseling
into *shalom's* infinite possibles and extents

I.

Partuition
Germinate, Orient, Descend, Wither, Recrawl

LIKE MOSES,

I am begun in the ear,
and the nested nesting of pyramids.
With the youth discontents of poetry
and poetic youth,
driven by its gale to the slop pits of philosophy,
making a lot of love and doing a little war,
and come home like the prodigal son
to a full-soul's rendering
of a merest fiber in reality's heart,
experienced as the briefest sharded moment of time.

That I may not write of my pain is evident,
but may from it,
to spot its sources,
and name it in my own perch over its depths.

In this,
Christ's eternity is held and released.

ACORNS

this strange closeness to the continual presence of the God who never fails even in silence:

I
When the sun comes close,
and acorns molded in wax take the shape of rivers,
so this by unbound words seeks to express my unbinding.
But only as dribbled like papery air sparked to flame may we thus,
for others to be unbinding sustains flame
by staining shame's flaxen pelt with a guileless nude burnish,
shimmering at sun while
others' scheming forearm sends crumbs flying, their diremptions
feasted like fire, torching through gut and gland,

portals to destiny shutting.

II
Symposed wicks snuffing,
I try hammer and planish these waftings mine:
"Away from me all men of violence,"
Rein all talk of destiny's rein!

III
When the early sun comes close,
and acorns molded in wax take to jousting at air,
I burrow away loyalties corded by lies
that engraved with another's, its nests of silencers
that had twinned our wills' as feared demons

Of icy greyclouds, synapsed with Brownian pricking and startled
boots claquing, coming
concer/ited to furrow blueberry moments against time's bloom.

IV
When the sun comes noon close to flash understory to wonder,
and acorns molded in wax cap soil with a forest walk and breast a navy's masting,
They rune memory in amber,
their plant intent to bone valleys
As now in myself broaching once again

by hollowed eye their leaf to find

and join the nexus of spotted, unkempt fall.

Decay challenges patience in eyes of all

As grace lingers its jab surprise.

V
Three-day through a dervish horizon's compel
To bed away, asway, and as a way from
tabernacled bereavings, my integument jibed and by strife's mirror furred
like moss eroding stone and
pu/ommeling toward fortress.

VI
By penning shadow's womb
I came only
but to vanity's hazening as await the crystal manner of reset clocks
that I could ring for you and daily renew,
coursing the steady bow against strings that
cage mercy, to hive instead with combs spiced of aether

by dew-filled nostrils of grace, turtled

as songs un-rote
against the rotting, the head-for-head, the daybroken.

VII
When the later sun comes near, to spring's surcease,

and acorns molded in wax take back the coursings of rivers,

prospect moments that lap each daybank,

ceasing hovering atop you but slipping, slipping now to feel its shouldered neck call, to particle reverse of course.

VIII
For such I have
from travel's halt relaunched
And by its river muscling sleds of acorns
dance their memoried lip upon heaven's beforing careen!

SHEMA

Spirit kindles the ear
to fuel with atmosphere ramifying,
with the soft peals of a gifted soul's throat and laugh,
angel embers that firework
like dandelion seed blizzards across the watch of the night moon,
to dew the dawn like sparklers,
to effervesce with grass,
to rear greening and greenward inlay,
their resining sequence propagating trust,
resonating merit.

To the bereft—making its sugars are not enough,
while to the aware and aligned,
its abundance broad ranging, keening compel.

Retorts lenses its gifting,
the keel that for some
is the bank statement's beguile prisoning—
honor's lard, the self-mantra'd, hoarded and hollowed,
to stumble sure, hallowing swells that bounce
temple to belly, up against cisterns of history,
in which we find its feather:

Noah's 40-day year in Provenance-accompanying the
amphorae-laden dove,
as vessels and cushions,
our ark's planking, irony's unmanacling,
reskinned by hail,
its electric gale coarsening
in a determining con-test of heart.

Shema's a priori of the ear-enlisted heart

resolves noesis's swirl and chaos by grace sagacious,

and by its proem of the heart's double intentionality

resigns Kant's whist to a shadow shut shallow engrave.

The haven-ward wind ballasts our heels,
jibs its pulse,
then, only then,
to come to know our familiars,
and square their scaffold
with this stubbling acquaintance
that partners as it soothes.

STRANDED MID-SWELL WITHOUT BISCUIT

I dream the dream of old men:

The dream of language to embrace like a wailing wind.

To dance the hummingbird resonant in you.

To swallow the wine dark of you,

to crunch out your shoulders and elbows the endless,

the rainbowed rossignol flight.

To float my cheek—this provisional atom's rhyme, a hammer that failed to mourn the nail—

on the cream of your belly.

A tongue unchains when with creation's align,

Like a meteor sap from throbbing sunsets

to bonfire spark laughter,

a speech yours and mine brushing from these cataracts

Grace's emergent landfalls of tears.

GRIEF'S PASSING

Trauma is ostrich moult,
a head-sanding poison gradient,
still-birthing to the saltant—
the hummingbird heart and kestrel eye now shrouded by walling's wail.

Grief comes:
as winter's yanked river,
Cataract-blocked and swollen-faced,
entire-world burdened,
like Atlas, a chaining absence.

When hot tears at last
claw my molar-clamped cheek
to leak into ambient indifference,
Jagged ice floes carry the rock-braided current
to pierce by morning a haughty temple brow.

Crumbling the numbing hardscrabble, this temple
into shards of slate
no scribble can soak,
no hollowing laments daubed,
No sigh dribbled, no sob's harrowing released.

Yet, a jibing dawn to this bone ridge kisses,
her hoar-brushed eyelash windowing snow-pillows
piling against leaf-slushed banks.

A reel and slough of God's frosty miniatures
comes to dampen this raven's forest pall—
to shimmer endlessly inventive and precise,
nonpareils to whirl and updraft hover,

fragile individuated atoms beauty-soldered as they near,
into an earth-collected, jeweled autograph.

The abiding bitterness sieged by
God's heart deeply buffering comes with news:

An eternally-etched and evanescently-forged promise.

Even cold's noiseless serene invites:
that in winter's sleeting sleep may tranquil dreaming find,
and cameos of melt wake to bubble seaward!

How much more for those roused to green the springtide?

In spring's certain arrival,
when from groans to hymn
the cadent lee takes eternal stirrings,
and we partner to the mast of sailing grace—
trimmed as by a dove-captained curtain,
by an ever-renewing, ever-repairing course.

BILLET TO SAVOR

Draw faint the pen, its fountain echoes
of (t)error and pain!
Your pillars muse of shadow birthing shadow
In lullabies of owls over barren grain.

Spurring disgrace's epaulet,
The dandered shoulder that rejects my dance-fingertipped invitation,
Where hope and peace have long lain slain,
Victims of ergodic myths leavening chance.

Yet endlessly inner ponder impossible commands:
Create, dream rebirth!
Only the head's fly-buzzing cradle,
My hands lamp-lit, their slumping distress chairs await Eos' cracking

Into the ever-dimming day,
History's ruin tracking.

A neck-scruffing brilliance takes the skies' hold—
Artifice, erst uncomprehended,
Now lightening recollected,
Discharges plastic surprise resculpting its story bold:

Not in death's origins,
These bones may live!
These sere vainglories halted,
Spirals and sojourn through.

Casting not insipid chaff,
But in rough voyaging—
Charity and caresses give.

To cease scoping aim of the moon,

And take the panoramic hook

Aligned with grace,

grabbing the recked for comedies now runed!

FREEDOM'S CREDO (MARK 2:21)

Who for Plato's sacked harbor intend,
Cicada-sanded and vinegar air expect,
Against grace's headwinds vainly beat—
Who by red morning vapors from a box to box emit, note:

The lily dances with eagles,
While dandelions denude golden borders
Like choral blizzards relentless,
Embracing the voided sediment
With nonpareils, the sap sparking new eras
That melt into eternity,
Bearing nuggeted Gabriel, settlement:

Poetry: a people's scar—
Shoveling from the paths of children
Drifts of slave-fueled sentiment.

APOPHATIC THIS DRAW ARRAY,

such beauty shifting
Battens my imprint to tongue electrocute, against
Claiming its life fulfilled, not by sharp-sated desiring!

Reef my heart, sir, mid-mast it!
Nail this brig to some other deck—
That I jibe away, this gale,
This siren recollecting—

In a clanking halyards' haven,
Like a wind finger's tapping out
The sea's pulse of forgetting—
Hips hushing like shells jammed shut, as now
These convalescing lips, telluric—

Until both wing open
Raw eternity's anon.

(Luke 1:8–20)

FOUNTAIN OF BLESSING

After the water, Jesus emerges
To image the descending dove.
Spirit where water meets
Rage, her air hovers ever swaddling purpose.

Who crossed the boundaries of Gilgal,
Joshua's conquistadors reconstituted God's incarnate—
Exiting from agencies to vanquish, so now by
Grace's gentle pressures to sway against appropriation.

Gasping, blood-unblock surgent cells to meet what is tent—
Jesus comes to such hearts,
Sensibilities turned from tractor paths of trauma,
To bring forth, like winter apples:

Beauty's whole and freed.

Wild death-in-birth, this uterus
Conceives deathless worlds without end from
The liminal mother's encompassing will—
Her breast the evicted refugee, suckling under extinction's threat, yet
From the barking gate at Rhea Silvia's trauma,
Released and now in joy cooing.

Water and atmosphere:
Heaven's strutbeat, rainbows
Rounding us into the earth's essence of renewal, infusing
History's wide avenues with
New families flowing along grace's eternal sunlit stream.

The wails of the newly delivered give way
To mother's joy singing the

Astounding punctuations of this living moment,
Washing our ears' archive with these glad anointings, returned as:

Christ becoming all-in-all.
Do you not see?
Spirit diffuses forth,

As a heart's move, eternity's astrolabe encompassed
Bringing the intended home, in

Glorious physical quickening,
These chimes of praise—our
Bliss rings out theophoric heartbeats—

For Nazorean comes to recradle Caesarean,
Lamb to turn the wolf,
The overjoyed comes to the violated.

We, who *"shall go out in joy, be led back in peace,"*
Mountains and hills bursting into song,
All trees of the field clap their hands—
All-in-all without end.

PATHING A DOUBLING BLAZE

That *ruby-shouldered trout,* fountaining and torqued against your gunnel—
Does charity capsize?
Now so silhouette your shock, like *smoke from a doused fire,*
Your fraught eyes a mirror set against my nature?

Might instead this disarraying, *caught and gasping throat,*
Be slaked by mercy!
Retire me not (as did that one pastor's daughter)—
I am not experienced for cruelties.

Search these depths for fizz's track,
That t(r)ailed red-marked, *flooding, that broken caress,*
Not *glassworked combustion.*
Pry open your heart for the pearl set there in our laughters.

Recall the *bridge and sap of dreams*
In the camps and canals we shared.
And forsake not your sense of *kindling the braided flames*
And paddling these braided sluices—
To reseed in us for the echoing knit and baths of love.

II.

Landfall
Songs Discovering Ruptured Earth

Aftermath of voyage by the baptized ear; emergence from stone, transition from disorientation to turn by a liminal but revelatory encounter with new ground.

MUSE(UM) [MAY 13, 2024]

Clutching at balance by a steady throat and ruby muscled heart
darning the hope of words,
to flutter them like butterflies against your eyelashes and cheek.
Where once set concrete and silos of acid gaze,
diamond-tip rotors scoured Thor's calendar for its ear(ly) of sky.

A striving order's *tarkus couture by viscera in dreams of plantation,*
Which iron gates its seiche of sugar and decay, an arrogate,
A raw communal ache for heaven's rage and malice, as satyrs
Gale their cobbled tinkle masks.
These *nincompuleant whinnies mine now windchime spectral gambols,*
Tuning and jabbing out a march for an absent band,
As the bitcoin synaptic sky darkens.

A poet sheathes his world in the secrets of his traumas,
His epee his thrust, an eros turning back its tides of erosive
Foams ever about the mouth, the sudden rictus of expiry—
That science ever studies in its preparations on trays,
Like mirrors to its grinning piercelamp:
Life's riddles solved through the studies of the frozen death frame?

How to still dark dream and shadow pull by the doubted page,
A pen?
A claim from the leaf arrogation by seep's ink of green, resonating for the

unfurl of the necessary, its fiddlehead arrival of futures?
By the deep knowing that beauty cannot but shine inward through

where its miracle unwinds

And to know this of your singer:

Search for leaflight quaking,

semaphores of spirit in the trees' abiding,

Like prisms beneath the paper,

And crumbling like the crunch of autumn underneath boots' confound.

THE BELL EPOC

From the restless to the relentless:
the age of bells ringing intensify—
sleighbells to doorbells
and phones invading our parlors,
mobilizing our intensities,
rousing us from slumber
in the expectation of novelty
and admiralty balls.

And now,
no one comes to our doors
expecting welcome,
no one rings.

And if they phone—
first by text, inquiring.
And if the old, out of habit, dial—
by a programmed theme identified:
no surprise there,
nor its expectation.

And if the caller isn't known,
we calculate
in our cushioned chair
whether to dive
into tight pocket
and pick out—
to open like the clam . . .
or not.

All done listlessly.

We hunger for restlessness,
for tentmaking,
but anxieties
have walled us
in a roundabout cathedral
of beeps and summons—
to ignore
like car alarms in the night,

the smoke alarm battery
shrieking empty's impend,
like a baying dog
at the door for potty
rather than society.

To visit any new kitchen
that beeps for what's new:
the idiot light
festooning our fridges,
summoning our glance
to its call to consider slow,
rather than pup
jumping up
toward the source
of dance's gut essence.

Idiocy of beeps for the cybernetic Logos
is but our shipwreck bridge rattles,
refusing the tiller's steady hand
as gales rush up—
t(h)rilling.

LISTERLESCENE™ ABANDONED

Tympanous mystics, these salad days dance Twilight's Concatenation:

"The clatter of looms in Manchester, the rattle of the machine guns at Langemarck—"[1]

Prepackaged proportioned sandcastlers of eternities:

"Eternity will be beyond the contrast between night and day, sleep and wakefulness. It will be a dreaming awake, or a waking dream, a perpetual twilight that is also dawn."[2]

By Analogies dreams mastered to throw off

the shroud of anxiety like

ivy wrapping ourselves shadow potted.

How thirsty makes such saltants!

How the wave zippers by a coursing effervescence

Code the shark's dorsal fin

on death's shorelines embracing twilight,

Ever twilight searching, measuring, diagramming

---

1. Ernst Jünger.
2. John Milbank @johnmilbank3, April 22, 2023. https://twitter.com/johnmilbank3/status/1649739774360469506

By which to conjure a sip of toad spit

dawn time's Anodyne

ripener on close-out.

But winter's expression miniatures the radiating snowpack

as sun and hoar frost kisses of morning,

in snow apples smiling from the shadows of the grey hedge of sleep, its twigs

as the January noon sharpens

toward the evening's icy ringed moon to the ramparts of snow

that endows a child's Christmas eye.

These winter's light spinning, squinting, furrowing our heels.

DERIVATIVES

I come to another riddle,
I call it irony really,
sounds more capable
of paths diverging and no guide
save the same epics that have set generations
to denuding thereby gelding these fields.

To my left,
the swamp of cement rot creatured
by rusting machinery skulls,
[lieu]tenanted and Tyrannosaurizing;

to my right,
the plastic and sludge-filled sluices,
which taking the match struck to the night crystal come
a pyre of fossil hope's falling
like frost huddling to greying's ash.

Of these, some burnt archives arriving
by these same faces, their pens clotting.

How dare we, stuck
in crooked-making spines of repeat!
Yours, mine, different only in make and model
but makes no difference to the commute
or the cavetrack—

a phonograph where the scratch halts the playback,
a scratch eternal,
an itch we ever claw to (t)issue violates
that soothes by uncooked and inert stoned sense?

This is the zombie iron frankenday riddles parade,
drum majoring over and over the scratched repeating,
these same field blends
to begin back at the beginning
to arrive at the beginning

which was and always will be
an act of fratricide.

(Until that brother comes to forgive…
how might that work?)

But my forehead patellated to silence such recurrent hiss:
not only where is the phonograph that
distends history, like a maggot-ridden and scooped belly,
but who absconded after setting needle down?

Who is responsible for not changing the flow,
interrupted mid, walking away for us as
honeyed idiocy trapping,
gripped like a vise to ambered, bug-eyed dullness?

I demand (predictably) to speak to the throne,
Martin Heidegger!
I speak to demand his thrown!

Not a friendly chat, mind you.
No flatteries.

Wake up, Sir Gander.
By a kiss Yourself first:
Being is being has an absoluteness of certainty
that obliges, absolutely obliges!

But don't we all want to dream behind the curtain
and escape awareness of responsibility?

So Frankenstain me:
I want a diagnosis!
to share as you discover the ink-blind Determine.

Or at the very least his assistant,
bound ear-gazened pillow
and Bent-Hearted monk rickling David.

Or the manager.
Can he spare some time?

Anyone?
Hallow?
U There?
Icu.

VIRTUED DEF/VIANCE

Stuck in traffic,
Patience? The course of knowing all—
to sever issuing roots of shadowmaking,
imaging rocketry denies patience.
Combustion, sister, transcends
this swaddling basinet of bewilderments—
a planet alien to genius,
which rises at anything but what has come before!

And hospitality—
as well from the dedicated well
of identities CGI draw(l)s:
Who is my friend in dystopia's drool?
So to discovering, escaped,
launched luminaries from their Birmingham jailings—
their mimicked courage, their universals?
Never my routines absented,
in condemning oils smeared across my forehead
to splash epiphanies shredding their maps
under seascaping helm set adrifting.

In such recollection?
Of what nostalgia do I reek?
I'm survivor and escapee yoked,
my aches to the legacies of recollected me—
nor loyalty mine,
but telic energies stitch humanity
and its ontogenetic milieux
into the nonce-bearing cosmos of possibles.

The cement that flies,
unbonded and unsealed to arcane templings:
My muse alone drives justice to make me accountable to her!
How she sickles and strews,
how I fertilize and seek,
and who can claim the yield,
who can sup its fruit and dive deeply
into hot-shouldered juices of Nemesis,
her return the crust of karma
for misshapen language that distorts cities?

From which gale, our shouts
fight back her acid tides,
never to reckon the buffering silence
that strains children's starving,
and instead sing of heroes
with transcendent bullet aim,
to suspend animation—
awaiting the troops of our dead fathers
to address that goddess
with their sweetness of knowledge attained:

For are they accountable
for their stories of flying above
and behind the curtains of existence?

We wash in the last coordinate bask of sun.
New virtues are to be sung,
fresh nimbi of starsweats to be wrung,
and corrie pavements given tongue.

Praying gratitude's superannuation
may warp a coriolus for us
in recusing titans—
that dilute soups of most ancient rage,

Nurturing instead by creeks, tannined grasp in sweet root.

ENTELECHY (VALENTINE'S DAY 2023)

Sun sear prodding the naked day (*you are my star*).
Both wave and particle, spirit formless opens dirt to growth (*you are my light*),
Soil *grace-becoming* (*you are my soil*).
Radiating civilizations of care, *Invisible God* (*you are my gift*).

Moon nights its light,
Illuming history's shadows ever-looping,
Fluxes toward dews and dawns never recurring,
Yet Solitary seeking in dim forms ever dissipating.

Reminding future's false crescent:
Torches of stoic old Artemis *never cast blooms.*

THIS IS A LAND WHERE TEARS GUSH

This is a land where *tears gush*.
Consider the lily reel, *air embracing*.
The resonant ambient valley recapacitates her gardening hue,
Visiting it gavel 'gainst the apex of cloudy mood,
Ever joined, asking: to serve the scar, or our scars to cease the service?

Twin butterflies ascend the green throb,
Their helical tag propelled as
The mirror of dawn, so posing this:
How will this day array, a museum's

Whitewashing mirror of listless,
The dibbled vase for a Banker,
Hands dibbled to cravat his lap,
Draining the field of concern except
To peacock ceilings?

Or in wild and stringy eyes
making capital to a neck naked under a sheet:
A bedroomed woman toward the half-curtained window
arches and cranes
As one drops a newspaper
At her knees, to become
The foot of the bed.

Into one limp hand cradled, her temple
too dreams of the golden-ruled shore limping, *imaged through another noon:*

Where sanding the breeze by appeasing the blaze,
Words are cicadas to them that hammer and repair,

Who see their traces in foundations recaulked:
Songs we share by sobs too.

And as by cedar boughs laid up against the bouncing hold,
These songs are hands cushioned, amphorae of oil and wine,
Baring scented shores, their supple intents swelled out—
Toughened and aged—and clutch reviving on

Landscape's resonant amber glow, its kestrel.
From heart to hearth and back again,
These our angels drink and feast too in
This land where tears gush from brokenness and delight.

I DANCING INTO WE

Overlay my body with middle-making soul,
Filling my flesh with falling leaves, quaking,
And attendant to the grasp of your crunch.

A fragrant smell of honey lingers on my shoulder,
My lips seek its source,
A buckler's ache where I bear your waist,
My shield against scrutiny.

My fingers rise to explore the sinews they trek,
The supine musculature of aid:
Your own tangling journey with the sun,
Glue to my pieces,
Into time's witness—an enduring, elemental push that pulls

From your imaging urgencies to
Array by caring's mete secret moments meet
That I find on you, pulsating into me.

We, a light-speed bearing symphony of gasps,
Our coupled, unwittingly audienced
Travel through dewy fields,
Our soles moistened to quench raging embers,
Sparked from sere twigs of other crook'd autumns.

Let us by spirit-captained verse step against effigy and stone

to ripple pond waters, and

breathe by their ever-widening to launching, like

roots for the hackjammer fountains of wildgrass

bursting through crypts and gating, to spy coming

Calendars, unreprised as new springs

like staves its sparkled seed, its purple and grey, attendant as music repairing,
These gifts of hope by simply your just and smiling embrace.

YOU, ME, AND THE ROCKING SEA

Dance is conversation among these three:

You me and the rocking sea

Night decks tumbling thread our joints

Sealegging morn's swayed cardinal points

As too these words reel and wobble

Our pasts leap up us to hobble

Purpose conditioned by not our pair

But always amidst the seascaped air.

HOLD, PARTNER, FOR THE DIP

Hold, partner, for the dip—

Is salvation a quantum abacus,

a large field of sunflowers,

a cosmic acre or more,

nodding in the galactic breeze,

and one slightly kens as beauty comes strange—

To dowse that prospect

moment by queening to stabilize

where mountain ranges would otherwise collapse

into holes of black night?

Darkness spewing in dew

the dawn like sparklers—

its justice fairly made,

if not fairly heard.

NOTICING THINGS

In propaganda's soot heaps prowls *nostalgia,*
seeking traitors:
spears thrust in backs knell the minor key,
an eliding unknown but certain to appear,
as by goatherds stutterstepping
to cauldrons, flamenco runways into voids.

Lashing Bashan's uptown
with foul air wafts, geometries of the minotaur's confound purpose
the labyrinthine studs of precarity and bony misery of history,
impossible by silicon to untangle, much less resolve.

Just asking questions too-on-the-nose:
"Thank you for your service"?
"I'm sorry for your futile youth."

Onto such gimlet eyescape sand

slung to popcorn the greasework canvases and bring to
jetty a dull duty of
art and religion, their flights to host
tragedico-ineffectuals and caesarian
wan and shadowy anguish proposing to guide and respire.

Just asking questions,
noticing things, splicing
until the parts fit how I want 'em together,
stuffing my holds and cavities
with cereals of polished absolutes,
set on my table and screen—
until typefacet of recipe comes.

That these drop to can drama and coat stage,
and wools its kin prick,
as goats unable to standaway
or pillow, or spark or cozen.

Noticing things,
not in stabiles to trust,
but in the futures made along our daily road,

where we vanquish dread

by soothing others the bond and rein appetite.
Our God is fed—
by alignment, not beliefing or rotes,
by sharing, not encrypting, or quotes.

III.

Sailing
Ten Crossings through Wind and Word

Motion bearing the between—pilgrimage, journeying toward another, traversing emotional and metaphysical waters.

RUSHING CHILD AND TAMING BREEZE

Irony-destined hypotheses—
Charybdis interrupted and domesticate—
Mete presents hurt outward:
their locked silos measured by them
and oiling salons' chainings,
sparked discord, never guide to rise
a hearth-(in)stead,
listless, stuffed, and garbage trucked sense to
map shadow solitary by cognitive touch,
not instrumenting weather's smog or the breeze,
such that revels by the absent and machined in which berthe I lie as
impaling.

Entrancing speech, rare languages as
sacrament comes spine-shivering,
companion-flooding chasms like
echoing brook' sinewed
runoff through the grated grit in asphalt:
This ebbing to my ear after
brushing the rocky canal of death
recollects prior passes by who gave me loin.

You Scylla,
my sail too has clawed at the clouds
like a lover gnaws her pillow—
in the loving sublime, not the terror or lofted or thunderstruck.
Marks the poignant share of haven hearth's sublime.

Rung with the rooster crow of generations,
nature's uterus kaleidoscoping its run-throughs,
where attendant Grace is peopled, demachined,

and boundless inner walked
and sent outer to water waking deserts,
repealing by leashing voids and tenting by the palm what litters and
teems oases.

A MICHIGAN TO MY LIPS (1958-)

Infancy found God's arms in another face, nature's my deciduous northland.

Not yet the people's face of Christ, but

woods, lakes, the snow, and breezes,

Still all presented, their bottomless bounties for wonder

Not yet cisterned and capped by adult privileging concrete:

Bullfrogs sang me to sleep with muted tubas

While the daffy hilarity of loons

Mocked hasty EosSuch dewy palettes of grace await, sleepyhead.

Hikes under Giant white pines along

A shallow stream, its currents braid through copper-colored stones plinking like gamelans

to reveal soul in motile energies—now

to reach coruscant turquoise, a lake,

My squinting leaps, now ever less furtive

at ripples swaddled and tickled by the hovering breeze,

Expose the sunkisst mirrors of midday.

Along sloshy bog banks stand

Formal elms, maples, and quaking aspens,

Signaling their semaphore to me: Awaken!

Sun-ovened pine needles and dank myrrh mushrooms, their whiff pry my nose to sense

the tingle when come the rains that tap tent flaps or drum bedroom windows,

Caressing my ears in the gush of life's fountains.

The crunch of autumn leaves by my unshoed feet, raked or let lay

Like the ground-belonging abundance of Mouldering apples to replenish the hearths of seasons.

These too God embraces

Earth bodied in me.

Endlessly inventive and precision-forged frosty miniatures,

non-pareils to whirl and kick in small flocks of entrance,

at the individuated fly my delight such earth-collected like what dumped beauty

and autographed, by every single jeweled evanescent—

cameos in winter's complicit and disappearing matters, bringing

Spring!

Afternoons outside, lily-puffed majestics

cottony wads of cloud sailing on the breeze , ruffling my windbreaker and hair in their wake.

Inside the vivid blue dome where I lay prone

in head-brushing meadow grass and milkweed cushioned Reveries,

Experiencing the sky and wind coaxing the arts of awe's poignant intrigue

As they whisper that we are friends:

Embark into the sublime voyage of grace.

Awake anew, To the other face of God,

Whistling its gentle breeze,

the child's enchanted sensory privilege,

Recalling us to wonder and gratitude boundless.

Ever filling us with gift.

HAIKU SEQUENCE

from a Greek verse fragment [Sapph. fr. 42]
Love's gaze rattled me
inwardly like a mountain
wind undresses oaks.

Setting course across
the old man's face gingerly,
the fawn-spots of age.

Back Dimples (June 8, 2023)
Rain rustling petals,
we shy common glances steeled
'top shoulders heaving.

Bobbing in droplets,
flowers dancing in the rain
as rustle these hands.

To sight foul or fair,
zipper waves play at sand's home,
building castled grace.

1 Kings 18:41–42
Go up, eat and drink;
heat heaved, ravening storms loom
for your corn, these (y)ears.

Tactics' grease and talc
hasten from talks of order—
keep watch on such vents.

Worries start to build:
Maybe meet for a movie?
Wonder if you've left.

Nature's museum
Ecotones reflect floods of
flowered vases we
miró-rs echoing

Tu es Petrus
This redoubt of rock
divine emplaced me invest
to reign like David.

Headlamped grills onrush,
inside we crane agreement—
wide smiles performing.

A BULLET'S DURRUTI

Who gallops with Valkyries,
Done in with a vengeful spear,
the stepfathering maw of reason,

I sing of the bullet that felled Siegfried Castellano—
his trireme measure ever—
unhappy destinies hijacked
by post-mortem's penning,
triggering finger to bolster knave-holds
ever plush and ensconced in comeback,

Aimed to ram into shadows heaven's gate,
And shard and sleet,
In heroism's grin and twist,
the ginned cyclamate to smell salt sleeping spring
and resurrect his summer's disgorge and corn
of hot nostril iron snorting smoke:

Not by talc and brain,
this destiny greased by ratio's gritty kiss so,

By autopsy as incantation refined,
And whip assigned:

This Bullet's Durruti
Climbs the guard of flaming angels,
over our walks in a telluric cauldron,
that bullet lands a bane walk,
scopes it though we Durruti's funeral cloak array,
a cleric's disguise wagered.

To feed the bullet song of
such hero's procession:
How triumvirs grasped your cold and unmasked hand!

Anarch redivivus by these shapeshifting reports,

Do bullets that cover priests in peasant backs land?
It can only be so! Testify angels of ballistic conceit as sublime,

Who ascend to plant re-guides,
autopsies of heroes,
sherpas these allegations like
from good guns to gin the skin of ravens
biering above.

A tombed family plots the clouded future circumcise
As we cut open our evil's interpreter
and tap sword to its shouldering over and over,
To snip Autopsy until it pastes as scripture—

To repowder Durruti into fork's Intent and land,
To lair its myth and husk in backs, ever turning over dirt.

AFTER MACHINED CONFESSION, ECCLESIASTES 7:10

Silicon's chew sickles futures, entrusting
connoisseur of warrior logic
to gin back our deadened fathers and their illusions they trusted.

By cold means sculpted in probabilities,
we'll doubtless conjure luck.
Death-assembled data sluice through the black water libel:

War terms our trade,
our fools' reach to advantage,
so its surcease is impermissible hostile.

Rather than give and leave our better,
such lucre-seeking code will grind street corners into

Mountain hands spread wide
against the horizon's advance,
mass-embracing and monocultured to
cultivate the taste of ash—
so hungry for machined aspics—
unspied metrics of craving bodyments.

Can any math the daughter of probabilities churn
Christ becoming all in all?

Can you not sure this fecund field,
its stalking thrust,
flowers to staring tank barrels
at Brandenburg Gate, at Tiananmen?

A flower's embrace that gums up the ape,
lowering the fragments of gravity into the wash of play.
An Easter egg wallpapering your labyrinths, hollowing such plans?

> Ecstasy draws me beyond myself, and in its wake I follow—
>
> not away, but toward myself, outwardly unfolding.
>
> In this, we recurse our project upon reality—its taxing, ironic ennui—
>
> and seek, by freezing, to form what should remain flowing.

So where is your algo Christ?
By what gate does he enter,
and by what trough does he repair us?

Relentless, he enters to scope and scale such—
bringing to flowers
a robe of golden and purple,
ascending angels ever visible to children.

THIS BARK MANACLING

Barques maniacal at
clowning storms unleashed—of confinements uncalming—
to deliver hence this bark:

> *Can this sail's integument, such fabled blousing,*
> *signify any sea's path to excellence?*
> *Can I sport, may I drink the blood of another man's risk?*
> *Or make another do the same?*

Unanswered,
then let not us hoist the sectioning shade of Caesar,
Marduk's meet with chaos to teat its torn birth, tearing,
And Shiva's grave tango—
narcotic, confused footed floateries—
to serve this spur that wakes by words
a culture's hypodermic dime, its com-bust, its security that lures.

No, rather

the fluttering kite, aligned with the dove's
our spine, gentling by up and down concord with haven's prow fizzling,

to become the flower and sap, their unyoke from every glintering

but the Sourced waves at hand.

INVITATION TO THE DANCE

Your glance dives,
dragging my waist along:
hip-motorizing me, those eyes so motile,
sidling me and you all over—
and insist on *wristing knowledge*,
to essay by grip and slake if they,
by prophecies, croon
necks of coming deep,
its *tempest both icy and melting of message.*

A single wisp of green golden wheat
settles with the paupered fields
in dew's caressing—the soil dappled sun,
pink-orange fawning
like chalk to story the captain's trot(h)
and make the food that gives its all,

as we tomorrow away.

THE POSTMORTEM OF POETRY

A book's index ribs atop its civilizing:

Is there entry for the just rule of grace—

For the golden rule?

If not, irrelevant its book as its civilization comes, doomed.

By retribution's jawboning is backshadow's anachron redraw,

score settling for negating g(r)avels—

for all they sought was timeless,

and to jumpstart there an absolute now prone,

where granite outlives, ever document

drawback horizons.

Which has standing?

The volcano insist patterns take,

or the lava scope which data break?

In the gullying and swelter

interrogations of poetry mark the course

where subject and object battle—

as the stubbed toe broaching a shutting cattle gate,

a narrows of the crooked rush

against by low deed

to chest mercie's incise.

Which genitive thus acts?

A poet's interrogating or interrogated?

The answer finds our essence

in these courses of battery and grave,

graved, graven merits—

For except by worldlies,

every "post-" comes prowling—

a gritty square of geometry and vertigo,

suspended in not-knowing,

howling out its last proprietary tones of ration:

So come now we rest on wreckers rusting,

to find a seat in the shaded courts

of rockets fading

which to Etna's buried sight still beam.

Etna holds fire not for ash's grammar sown,

but to speak child—

weaving peripheries' dust

into w(h)ig-determined history,

where blood's forgetting drives

the hewn poetaster reck,

the gnarled wasp of bureaux flecked with

strategy.

IN NEED JARS MEMORY, MY CHURNING

For time's po(e)tentate such leaves-taking
draws out Sabbath from regret by odes to craft:

> As mustard flower's yellow titrates the sky's dripping blue,
> Cedaring green and blushing grape,
> So mines the poet silence for filaments of grace,
> By training teasing out filigree for
> Christ-lit budding, figlets of imagination
> Come to spreading like yellow-shining
> Beacons toward indestructible harbor.

Where ripened and succulent is churning the merit
to sweetest aging—

So *get up and get going*—it is the quarter's century's Epiphany which
comes cold fog-shrouded—
wrist resolve by keying the motor and drive

to turn with voices joined through hope
praying as feathers shed of
an arrows' aiming,

despair's unraveling.

SHAPE-SHIFTING TISSUE, HIS SCHEME

Shape-shifting tissue,
the petrolated, charnel scheme—
a complicating sort he cored by tongue's
unhitched plow,
face's toccata of rejection—
an earthshone moon skins it by outline.

Not overcoming himself
until by virtue late composing
what so prolonged delayed:

His marvel—
a sun fused by rehusking Spring rains,
such harmonies into the sweet tasted dawn.

By what glimpse escapes the press of grapes,
and so ever comes to these skins
the seeds of sing
into time's flowering wonder.

IV.

Mirrored
Human Refractions by Theory

By the turn of poetry, fragments cohere not as answers, but as reversals set as accompaniment—contrapasso—for new storied courses of grace.

TODAY'S DATING ADVICE

Wish I'd thought of this decades ago:
NextDoor a free give-away
of a substance of personality—
like, say, an old wine shelf.

Spy your porch from behind
your intent's curtain
as your proximate
wrists its offering.

Then come out—
like the Sheriff of Nottingham—
to conversate about varietals and vintages,
unspooling straight to the King's own court and chambers.

Or such essence of inline skates,
kneed love's redlining stumbles—
a drawer's put toward crockpottery,
or rusty fencery.

You get the idea.

Pro-curing, and freed—
as a s(h)elf found,
cellared for another's keep.

Follow me for more tips:
about dressing for levity and sport,
about such uncorking crafts of
choosing being chosen.

And, at least,
emptying a garage
into someone else's basement.

DRAGO(O)N'S FEAST

Plaited thick with delicacies, this symposium—
with courtesies and rhythms
to sate courtesans and climbers, by these laws:
your comforting, liturgical ornaments.

Torches cast at marauders, gates closed against
children aflame with genius,
to sweep, fork, and repel
down the impaled and the impaling.

How are the dishes to be put away?
Is the detritus of chipper eats sponged clockwise, toweled in reverse?
Scraped and bucketed? *Does it really matter for us?*

As a chameleon jewels her hostess,
no doubt some future will implicate my cheek in her rouge,
bedraping cameras whirring—
we all know it, *fealty requires it.*

So we cartwheel through this sumptuous night out,
with a smooch to ourselves,
and strafe and style toward a next too-early dawn,
its raze and razzle—

with absolutely no idea whose high sun
will lipstick the next noon—
but a face of noon nevertheless.

What a fraught climb we ever weasel to weave!

AS I NOW VIRGIL GUIDE

I sing the prosthetic-armed man
who disengages from Ares' charnal schemes:
beached hulls smeared with timber and expired soul,
a sea's sputum that frothed and slimed—
this assembled rictus,
a grey sand testimony in the story-scoured ribs of skull-less whales.

Who reshores in Dido's blooming fields,
Ceres magna de abolenda Aeneide,
ceasing the harvest of orphan tears,
cisterning instead saltless springs of dew.

To summer paint hazy sunshine's clutch,
clutching the beans of tomorrow's grace,
seiches of amber embraced by cream,
from the plow's worn prow rising.

I sing of multifarious men—
much-wandering, much-turned—
abandoning the gates and corsets
of maidens battle-girdled by
deceitfully allured lips,
spitting only death's hoarded treasuries.

Oases surely discovered after sunken sere shadows,
Maskils, history's goodness,
awaken us to multitudes repairing this way,
with epics-fractured souls annealed by hymn and psalm,
and supping and sipping with enduring meals.

Cruel seascapes companion greedy rusticates until
when they find their own rotting timbers
in un-destined harbors intend,
and this dead caked *contrapasso* wash away.

CRUCIBLE OF REPAIR

My youth stranded wild mountain pools,
living long TV expanse as Grey habitus,
under the sphinx of a turning sky, a sky that
coughed out the day, curtaining its wick with the smoke against Orion,
where I, his flaming spear of dusk's birthright,
besought to braid compasses to new bronze.

I came to hitch to regiment,
its machine eyes spun to destiny.
I attained the wolf's mouthed tail, ravening teeth veiled,
the emblem of Ouroboros,
statecrafts that set eyes upon flags
priapic, staked by soil, bloodying camo lifting up by the bootstraps.

Against which I whelped to limp out denuded sensories,
manacled ideals reworked as the Real,
their vain prospectus for the hooting moon eclipses
of awareness of what astonishes:

Until these lips found, as by a staggering bee stealing honey,
earth's hot waist in weather—a shield, green and deep,
though stained with rusting illusion now, the living and clearing hand.

Spirit exploded the enigma of dust into the imaginatorium
of stars' other folio.

In season's discovery, ours now—you and I—the healing,
energy, gardens in the breeze, and magma calling to the deep naked light,
twitching aspen leaves mirroring over a pond's twinkling,

I run my fingers through your hair as
tenure these painted ardencies witnessed, to carry
this crucible of repair and resending
into the *grace-purpled blaze*—sprouting dawn and pipe over the mute sphinx
with noon's eternity, attendant harmonies candid and unsorrowing,
singing the straitened human essence.

MEDICINA ANIMAE—PATRISTIC LOGIC

where healing precedes

even the wound's

awareness of itself:

A metaphysics of repair

is bilateral relating,

bringing bilateral suffering,

expressed first subject-activating

and then experienced as objectivizing

and maturing into vice versa

(imputation they call it):

by the doctor first,

and the accident second.

Then in accordance

with the prior relationality:

the soul first,

then the body (1 Peter 4:1).

As awareness grows,

snail-like in shape and speed,

from natural,

nature-(w)recking acquisitiveness

into a trumpeted consciousness

of a higher world

and its non-negotiable higher demands

of Golden Law,

the soul enters the struggle

with swanning sin

which brings its own sigmoid of pain—

as jolts of sorrow and reproach.

After sin extinguished

by faith in salvation

and alignment with its archives,

a soul potentiates

to scaffold eternal essence.

And then, the soul's encheir-ing

investigation by the bone of soul cracked by eros,

which too brings its own pain,

in this somatic by nature

toward the body's practice eternal.

Which so becomes by transfigure

the lambent embassy of Repair itself

to those of nature

still imputed to enter.

CODEX CARMINA VIRI-TUDINEX

Dominiorum latronum
fautor fasces
praxis patronorum
manus vini panisque tradens
et per amorem rubescentis in sanguine:
vox urbana et pax burana

Fata paparum Anglicarum menti meae ceperunt,
So far from Shakespeare I learn:
these dons and cardinals and barkers
marked their (t)red.

    It is the trifle's icing
    that exposes the baker.

A BIRD MAY TALON THE SKY

to bear it away, but not so me the matter at hand,

the stages and staging of the sky stabbed

that emerges by our young

To meet everything else in its

complaints and sores

and frangent, uncompliant soaring.

To see as such, in eyes cobbled juices of shame and ken for hope

as if one could snap out from the infinite outside of time and space a
bony-fingered chunk of form and scalp it atop a small

box to sport with it, confident in the biasing of survivors:

I don't know where or when you are reading this, yet

how orthodox petty we scum mind and logic from

chaining tongues of hierarchs, unknowing that they meet the divine
heart training for a depot of obliging freeing thereby. . .

Not of the same claw and nail aberrant—

As the dead yet continue, Vampirically,

Deadening with the mid-19th century horrors re-roosting a new extractive range.

This the age of

Vlad the deathboning dataset

under sarcophagi of sun-setted data

and Dr. Frankenstein's pilgrimage to genius tearing apart

living wholes to jam together mixmatches of rage.

But it has happened! the order is overturned because the appropriating has been pitted—and recently at that, for

Such joy those still soaring, while time is at an end

for the crook too early strong manned by rents,

as the High Attribute takes the eternal seat in view of all (Jer 31:34a).

BIRD FEEDER FABLE

Beaks that hammer seed

make for bullies—

the small titmice, *Baeolophus*:

look not to them for poignancy.

Woodpecking ebon creepers of all sorts—

look not to them for thrift

that shovels and scatters

by streetsweeping muzzles.

That is but their phenomena of beak,

not their nature.

(Matt. 5:30)

And neither ours.

One that hammers,

or one that shovels or kneads—

these neither nature make

nor abandon.

But one that wipes a tear from cheek:

unlike the grotesquery

opening Malick's *Tree of Life*,

the fable of nature is not bullying.

To make of our lips

a hammer and shovel—

well, that's of essence inhuman,

a nature of appropriation.

For the restoring Adam,

begun as by same nature launched toward essence:

let supplicant imaginatoria

wake the blind stage, and manage a kiss

toward Christ.

LET THE DEAD BURY THE DEAD

We're their age, entombed—
gothic Pharisees and Sadducees,
of Draculas—
necking virgins, nihilism's target,
algorithm designers
ramifying deadening datasets inward
by canined ideas injected
of flesh as brain—

and Frankensteins—
tearing the living from their whole
to ship mixmatched members

categoricals and cauldroned mash,
lab partisans gone amok.

These, in fissuring Appropriative trapped,
tried glistening the Attribute
by Ambering flows.

Their world sensed
through the false Absolute,
making of mind a gearing.
of systems by geared transcendentals
working only toward the unintended—
and futile though

—Turing Tested:

Caught by a Biercian web

of slow-spinning nobs and sah'ibs

wending us to their bill.

To perceive differently,
we rise from belief in forms that have no beliefs
to heart-led centering,
energies and *kraft*
anointing peace,
reconciliation restoring destiny
from the institutioned and self-willed.

Let fall the past from our teeth:
systems imposing sense
onto seated, inebriate noise.
Let adventuring stimuli
expand connections—
our sense of now
at the street-address,
where wild chasms of necessity lie.

Let us fear's dissolution mete
from minds seeking
through the consternated
vantage and aperture to rob.

Recognizing instead worms, anxious resenting
as tabernacled stations
in the assay of life—
and realigning to living whole and wise.

FISSURED RUNWAYS

"I'm intelligent: I notice patterns,"
"My Spiritual gift is discernment."
Away from me, all workers of unrighteousness.

Living between the cozening
transcendentaries of molten dawn
and dusk's release of sighs,
over seas' reproach—
where resentment usually leads—

a green flash:
a rare launch of repentance
savored to land.

HIBERNETIC DISPATCH

Words raw
claw the ravening void,
their talons dig a collapsing hole in space
like a castle of sand set against whirlpools.

These vertigoes
from mind's despair
when knotted to heart's intent.

Like
rage-les in the clouds,
surveying by their married shadows alight
as through the slats of a fence,
espying old berried horizons,
futures titan-bent by brambles, unveiled as the sun recourse
and casts its unsheathing stone.

Consider to insider these,
our savories and accouter noised to make the man,
which wisely artisan battles by
thumb and forefinger nuances,
weigh(t)ed out in candles.

And so come worlds unattended except
closeting scars from games of hot poker,
ours to novel, daub, and campus them
with better disdain.

We've seen your man before,
jackdaw weary and bemoaning temples
of our children's prospects!

You weep of virtue never swept
by merit that survives the strafing gun and landmine?
Yet even fifth-column assassins who cannot even to wives confess—
look here! They tuxedo our opera boxes!

And now how You abide?
Except by prettying revilements
and red rump rubbing buffoons.

Failed Machiavel, sincere and earnest,
gamester now of arrogance,
gussied and supple in metaphor?

Much more blessed are earthfreed men
in the atmospheres that suckle our return,
by tinctures of bitumen and news tickers,
titrated by camo's high and holy nose!

Our abiding nipple of better inebriants
machine generations and tether
oases of oblivion's grey
to rockets and braver saga.

We've seen this type before,
with frayed threads stirred by currents of creation's deepening,
a needle eye by angle changes the moon!

The expect(or)ant of effables,
its poisoning anxiety: depressive, irritable recollect,
robbing our sense of hand and feet,
the tremorous shyness masked, its ungraving gaze.

A vomit, whose gums bleed with verse,
a hand-twitching mystic,

Poet you, OUR gate to troubadour corncobs and venture in,
For to make us your cozen?

Our bars will weed you from our classrooms—
and compost in acid strewn on the rocks such utterings

Theirs to destine detritus from aperitif banter—
like ashes fruiting atop ears' autumn eaves.

Such strange meter—minor-key sinew, pulsar-grimed ego—
scoffs out a hollow-chested toccata
to our planted chants that beacon our adventuring,

its tables swelled
into the fruiting bellies of the Peneloponnese,
spilling forth acorns of wit and boldness
from bedded oak and wine.

Stable, then, the galloping chalk of these muses,
cupidities of all who would bridle our necks
of steamy blood, as if our enemies' perfections, knowing
we may chisel advantage from Greek marble, and do!

Blueprints of missed opportunities from the expired
on which we wager and re-horse their ploy.

Thronged to amaze as one,
Our powers in the arts of expanding subtlement and diagnosis!

We know that massage and sandwich better make by other hands.

So bear and cross, such knowing song tears
into us no threat or openings.
And if they sprout, they have for our round up leaf't,
as too we have our adults reared and ready

as assembly-line handkerchiefs waving—
at your troublings to us
acrid weather woven,
and by our sunset to sleep with you

by pillows these our hibernetic forms.

THOSE BOOTS (102323)

Those pearl boots, earth-heavy, dragged Polaris down among us—
their iron-stained heels whittled my soul to a syllable,
its oyster sigh hiding under the canopy
of oaken deck-kneed hasps and
greying smiles alluring, cryptic, and subtle.

Such spits of new and tufted sand arise between us,
sifted by salt-scented essence to pry the relentlessly ramming waves.
Ours to measure the winter sea's gasping,
our wet-flecked journey becoming the fable
that torques and joints other passes—

of embrace ashore—Dido's *kairetic*,
her plowfield divorced of Mars' strew,
outside promising and distinctly left right.

V.

BC (1980s canēns)
Canon of Becoming in Bone and Blood Ascending

Liturgies of Inheritance: where biology bends toward metaphysics, and elegy becomes the vessel through which sacred time opens.

A DIVE (THAT COMETH)

Phase swallowed whole left shuddering by this kiss

Such an easy arrow act to become lovely water

And envied

Dissolved and remote until memory's lung rise various in columns:

Rhythms' burst to eyelids thus quickened

Now evolved, palpable atmosphere

Tilting in time to name your smile aloft

Gasping failure

Comes the sound below not risen

I thought my own:

A head separate, immiscible, and raining from the brow

As I once knew you.

NONE DOUBT SOME MANTID TRICK OF MEASLED NIGHT

by claim of delphi in misted streets alight:

as grips ring upon a van Go sun

chaplets of rain twig glass fingers unsponge each one

these nimbi wrought of starsweats trapped and wrung

along the corrie gurgled by sewer's tongue.

ONTOGENY

I

Treachery of calcium and phosphorus trace like frost etch the plasmic dissolve:

that the fishbone

arrow-asserted itself by

microns removed from

logic the sympathy that coughs that lobed-fin out.

II

Gives so lean an urge to nestle

in beach rock, those sizzling scuds

of ocean evanescing elegantly into wingless flickers

of burn.

Ill

Amphibian urges keen in the lips turn: altered valences,

the just account of vapors arisen

in and for the insist clowns of bias: Comes the shared wink.

IV

Now will habituate

the ductile screech and clack

at Long Neck/Sacral, then a chorus alight with syrups

song of attach, re

turn: bear the rattler cellulose smart of time.

CLADOGRAM

(As if the tree were still, and my young knee an eye to its bark:)

Scarred from shimmying up the tree-fort

of histories, academy in the boughs, litterers of the furious now with letters

to nature

As feathers flung; or unlike Moses' their tablets compost without fossil. Weightless

as remove of a leaf, its death-snap touches as upon kin:

As feathers flung; or into lint sensibility attach three, worded ascent.

Heft. Ur. Ochre.

Our cheated pain. Rippled tang—excited glaze comes of the slipping moment. Alone with

gravity for instants, never an age,

What can be so furious proved? Sweats. Cat-kin. Pilar.

Our cheated blood. Dear mythlets back as if from any but the gloss enormous:

When scabs do not heal so much as harden and vanish.

Winged. Loosened. Lonesome. Chaff.

Our cheated scars. Scars of men. Man of wounds.

A BRIEF METAPHYSICS OF MEMORY

The whole is mirrored, stymying words—
Scarlet striping on white sails reflecting blue,
When the shore lies miles from sight.
Lapsed engines of eloquence—
A breath of wind sets the sails billowing,
So too the hardening of a memory,
And the entrance for a new kind.

(A tribe unto herself, it is woman who remembers this.)
She lives, she remembers,
Excavating each memory of a prior guest,
Cheering them on as her own.
She remembers she will sleep,
And that most of her memories, like artifacts,
Will pass into another.
Even this memory spreads like seeds
On a savage wind.

And it is a man who remembers these words:
Temporality is an illusion; memory precedes existence.
Memory enters this liquid body,
With the sequence of extensions comes the illusion of time.
These are inhabitants, instantaneously alive,
Laying down memory in this husk, then passing on.
I am not I, nor we we,
But I am for a moment—vanished, replaced—
These machines, repositories of artifacts.

None can remember the enormity of the first memory.
The cosmos still recoils in horror
At that first mirrored skull,

Fashioned to combat the ennui.
Into that skull, many imagine a cinema—
Dumb lights and bartered hues,
Reflecting without pattern.
But as the random lights shot into every crevice,
Something seemed gaudy,
And the aperture closed,
Snaring the aboriginal memory,
Like a just-closed eye marks wraiths of light.

Jealous of our possessions, we must be—
They give our flatness depth,
And our loneliness a course of arrivals.

Four dreams, checkmated:
The dream of protracted youth, undone in the mirrored skull.
The dream of Apollonian vengeance, shattered by reason's fragment.
The dream of Dionysian energies, slaked by fleets of wine.
The dream of Christian peace, trembling before Abel's first wound.

Whose dreams are these?

HIGH-SPEED PHYLOGENY

Such

gravitas in the banking, this metalled

smile of performance—such centrifuge; and I come

aged, skinned with seat-leathers, a turtle of deep draughts and innards-wan, jogging

my manner of collapse ashore, yet prelapsed and rare (amniote I, plying vectors

of fickle earth).

Now

with sharp terror yet easily I can throw over the wheel and bounce

aloft, like a trout torqued and electric in sunlit heartbeats, quick to rebank with a giddy spank

(and burp the substrate's uncease: the heady drags of solar abandon exhausts in guts of these

sighs—tensile jetsam, bubbles—this gastrulation of Moment, this Memory).

For

high-speed handling

the appointed interior, sac of humours shivering in the acentric drive:

senses recapitulating the phyla.

(SUPERCONDUCTIVITY)

Give thought a motor, advance in silence:
skirmishing the mien agonic
and throated through:
whence muscled flights concuss cheeks and
cornea, like bubbly toasts
to worries shared, and fated too.

At our elemental, then:
proprioceptive equilibrists of the foretold
and buoyant with amazed prides, then, to sing.

Yet entropy saps, malignant as heats,
and yearnings doused with draughts—
the wine-dark craft
dripping from our Aeschylean oar;
for each has in various evolve an idiot ooze,
this write to people the conduct eterne.

In arsoned grape a combust, then, to residue
the robes of dead, sawed life—
a colder organic, and erasable, too—
the suspension of works shifted in periodicity,
calm now in a web of simul-carbon.

Thence to true levities,
on platforms of opposing magnetisms,
our secrete modelled and fire-clotted
into brittle shells, mediate.

Lest a stumble,
museum these quick like Atlantean ceramics

and stretch the etiquettes their due,
giving motor to thought,
advancing in silence,
skirmishing the mien agonic.

SEMI-CONDUCTIVITY

Sparking quickly with its thoughts of day,
a glacier ghosts time's volumes,
without pattern or abandon.

Playing gauzed night,
the burning etch of orbit-junks
rains as from a piñata
(the busted myth of spheres),

Instant, applaused intents measured
without allowance:
by amplitude alone then
to render scenes to another grip.

(Divine the synaptic finance.

(Still, the snuff of constellation and bird,
and the poesy of g-delete
to aver kindly the heritage of matter.)

River of electricity—
is this the swim of fish in its eye of home?

SHORT BAHAMA

I

On the carpet of the arcane prophet—

    the Holy their only read—the pieties

    of mothers grappled

So that old men wear Hebrew names

    (unlike Joseph or his robe)

into a history where geneology shears

    the handful of surnames.

It is to science, and not to hope, for

    old men to carry their mothers' Bibles.

Without citation, where be old men?

Zabud, "the son of Nathan was priest

    and king's friend", neighbor to my father.

Mina his wife baked johnnycake and cackled

    as her powerful grip crushed ghosted

    frog-let which startle my father in the

Wash-house. That wringing of moment, that memory

    as of her wrist shaking fingered

Splay of guts outward: chilled at the

    saucy willfulness of this aproned

Old woman waddling her snicker back

    up the kitchen steps, my father wide

Eyes met mine to resolve in his own humor.

    'Some phylogeny', munching later

On the johnnycake she

Brung me over.

II

Ties like these, I grap at your memory

    like 'a-drowning.

III

All in all, a good thing that rain.

The cisterns be low, the tomato sad.

Only when the fruit lay exposed in his hand,

    round and ret under the gauze of membrane

    did he cease the exaggerated brutality

    of his movings. He had snappled off the

    citrus and peeled it with vigor. Squinting

    and swallowing as to stifle a protest—

    its acids ordained like an idea—he sat

down on a stump of palm. The gusts were

　　　building again, and the surf sang.

And he felt massive.

To the shivered surround, like Juney and an ancient Greek chorus:

Inserting thusly he thumbs its cavity,
　　　as if to part, as if to burrow
　　　　into its grave cell, amid as foliates time.

PALM SUNDAY, 1989

As when lacunae of event horizons merge their outside like droplets of water, shrinking
the balloon of matter, thus distorting the sky,
that archer is young again and upon the crane:

It is written (*Ephemerides 3.19*):
That time was washed
like cups and plates.

Each year I find less rock pulsed here by
frost, less of earth's
quoin emptied into the garden bed our
composts make, riled by
auxins that boil off all but the roots of
lettuce. I find instead

ellipses: pacing from the typeset
THAT finger-staining like
dyed wrists announcing burning chrome—
these foliated seconds grave error run
from seasoned council of Computus scribe—
motion—

Everywhere:
cycloids soiled
now

and

cop-per-y: *cop-per-y*: *cop-per-y*:
centipedes,

razzias of beetles,
earthworms napping like hound-dogs when I roll them over.

I claim their didymium salad:
peachstones aged and smoothed testes the color of nephrite,
skittering chaplets of acorns, clicking oak-flakes.
Dusted corn-cobs, like emptied typeset, curachs pitched of humus wine:

Fresh earth—little witness:
the peppery resins I take in like tears.

Against the front of altered spring, I bend to guide lettuce crystal beyond the gale,
into pattern sprouting—

the growth an astrolabe from two solar weeks, sidereal
gaps the clues marveled of new archetypes; then,
perhaps,

It will be a season for figs.

(MANTA A-WHORL BY THE FLEEING BURN:

an hour or more her cladistic dance.)

After I slapped the surface and secured the claw in eight feet,
I push up to squint,
where over the gunwale abeam the ray kept a belvedere:

Where kestrels her shadows amid ebbs,
where my skiff clocks fulvous with coruscant left
of the river of dusk.

Curbing a spiral when she chevies off the reach for moments—
covering always by the drifted beam—
decamped of this corolate bind as if a

visitant with need of tonic in the cratered yin/yang raches,
the gutted cays of ancient coral that lagune our forms.

Caducean, I am an ear at this chromosome shuddered of sillions in
rippled streams—
as cirric song: hers the cochleae-studded fettling
palletted of Homer and mine that wind and wind,
cerulean burls the memory we feather of brindled spine.

Risk ambivalents carry risk, she hums: *Ever hums.*

Straying finally from this charcoaled moment,
from her partial skewed flower as etched within
the parabola tide against light,

what she removes of geometry is finish,
the mystery as shies from the last coordinate wash of sun.
What remains chiral within; except what lasts:

Attaching the distance she series leaps of
arching stations—eight-foot leaps—each one
along a radius, each one a slap at
rippled surface, and each one a calculus of yaw:
each one—and I aver they were many—each one by degree a flash of
nakedness; *belly:*

By crescents revealing its whiteness, by motion its name.

And I await each like the season: Awaiting each for its glow,
I await each by a moment.
I await each

As leaps she starts the night.

SEEN OF BURMA

Sandspit actually arisen against
campaigns which hoove these shallows:

Buffalo bowed like plows and peer-urging,
march slav rhythms onto the starts of a boy's green bo whip,
maestro of the subjunctive, this shirtless Hannibal.

Where spread out daily to pass the noon like penitents,
these garments still against the piping scurry,
selves of contemplation, to dry.
In the yet lonely distance, egrets like ghosts their reflections
feast on a disturbed river.

(Ghat on the Irrawaddy)

As the sun grows and moves like a lover,
the droning heats yet subside—

into the hum of dousing iridescence
to husk the smolder from this
golden hulk, this steeple.

To eon sighs, like exits, these:
an hour-long tender of bats,
ashes whiffling the thecal mists of dusk.

(Shwedagaon Pagoda)

Hairpins from Mandalay curve lids twice eleven up forty-two miles. "Up-traffic has right-of-

way." The geography reserves oil in plenty.
And no man-trade in spare brake pads.
Like fear, judgments arrive more easily.

(Road to Maymyo)

POTOMAC SEGMENT

Up from Georgetown, its estuarine flux within the Piedmont's last,

the sea shakes the rime of Appalachia at Little Falls. Beyond is

chordate river, as upon a spine of rock: messengering the ancient coruscant

come of sky-buttered sulci.

TRANSPIRE

Cauldron aligning each iron-

spun moment into its perpendicular: magnetized

by syllable, polar ribs stripe weft's cell

onto these airy tiers. Yet like life, breath

Peeks outward: Spills outward.

In song of some enfurrowed Druid to that

aorta of tree sucking on solstice

grey—steaming twigs like capillaries

distill the palpitant noon of its darkness,

into that which grows low and convex

as it finds the tissue of earth.

Like a smile come of nothing the sex

there is re-aging: the goddess glinting

vermillion beads dives birth

underground, her shrinking crone to the ruddered

hem of roots. Amid time, this swimmer,

this nimble nurse buoyant in her escape,

her youth—her laughing miniaturization

in surrender to the jailing filament

like from frost; but as a particle pristine

with quickness alembic the duelist atom of morning.

Tree, flipping, takes her ascent.

BOLETI

Unfamiliar amongst the cold floor seiche of rot, I loved

age-veiled alabasters, foundlings:

elbow, shoulder, thumb tasting of time and of metals.

What time I felt

the rustle

as smacking lips

as if

I tasted, too.

DALMANUTHA

(Flesh.

(Its portion is water in water. Dissolved.)

Anchor before truth, can this be synapse, too:

sunlit current sparks to its own; inconstancies, the unhabituated? faucets draining the reflected

lily, itself unmoving as if a ship among gales? (Anchor before truth.)

To retell, snatch and toss. Fat eager fish

Towards beaching seats. They rain of red splay amid arcs of frozen time

geysered from a scene of scale-razored

palms. Others named send eyes now and not until vapors like sleep

elide into the land of omens

and amens: that one enormous, collective blink (hiss-clipped Sanskrit, the death of place—catapulted into the solar exhaust

spirit like dandelion seed); such blinking as shears the flesh of history, its

molecular impetus. Such blinking as leaves the patent now shuddered.

MIND'S AUTUMN

Acorns unsought (thus believed)
of a late attribute plant of forest

Yields to mounds the great massed of ramenta
brittle as from faded air and inks;
great mounds of progress raked through stains of
cellulose—well like tangled words for paper—
a-snarl and bound for the burn,
propelled by strokes grounded and sure.

Each strained, crumpled senescence holden,
each failure, to leap toward
rite's duly roast. Yet of
those things that dog the tines like dandruff a comb:

Noisome acids in capture play,
biting like cancer to virtue
a rampant rig. And of those things that

Stream from the bouncing mess to settle in bands,
striping the feline with a green and moist sensibility,
that unsingable which marks by affect—
keep-safe locks, the eye's dart-claiming,
a sly and fingered eros—until that time as

Skills await to brush aside these streamers;
until then they arise like furies,
inciting to shades of blood and bile this aurora

Sleeping late in the summer canopy.

REQUIEM FRAGMENT

"Tuba:
birdsong in its arcs and

mirum:
ebbs like kanji

spargens:
were sound made inked, leaf

sonum:
densest calligraphy forged per sepulchral

regionem:
anxious of drown these Stygian greens,
startle suckings of grief.

Quem patronum:
Charged with indigos
now drowsy, full term

cum rogoturus:
of wit's time, self—

vix:"
(thus scored a score)-espied

Justus sit:
elegance, this ratioed succor

sicurus
of tames dispense—

these anti-hymns
of vengeance.

FEBRUARY'S LINTED SOLACE

to that bed he
had come to pass. He reached out as to grab of it,
the glow gauzing the windowglass.

I saw those times, his head turned
and mouth ajar as if to empty
the throat of pebble. Yet

save breaths of bedsheet
he strained silence
to cup hands into the trembling ventricle of noon.

The night of his death—afterwards—
I grasped at the daughter-in-law, and she at me, in
a crowd and heavy rite—I felt the ache as my jaw;
my lungs snapped to
corral each breath—

Like sleeping to forget.

VI.

Pillows Tossed
Arcs of Parting through Wounded Grace

Prophetic lament, solitude, grief, and reproach; Confession, metaphysical experiments with integrity.

DOES HISTORICAL LOGIC—

death-looming and—intending—

admit, simul,

of aperture

and aperçu?

It is drone-dripping shadow,

Machine moon and precise,

like Salome,

ever platens heads—

John the Baptist

becomes her gorgon.

O model desperately seeking spirit,

get thee to a noncery!

Skip stones across a spring-tide pond

and note smudges of geometry's office. Of source

brought to the slur of surface.

Withdraw to sand-scour junkyard's canyon

these melt-stained crayons and your-bloodied plate.

These from which to recanvas by dipping child dreams,

And by others to repair and see-write.

IMAGE THE MAN—

eyes that have wept,
ears that have heard murder
in the howls of a hungry child—
a mouth that's thirsted,
its cistern capped,
and her family's olive trees chopped and burned.

With scabs from suffering,
a heart that's been whipped,
a back that's bled.

Whips and scorn of luxuriating thorns
drinking blood,
the vinegar merchant's vampiric therapy.

But striving for new wine—
healed blood, its true and joy drinking.

By this inward, outside the camp,
we image blood outward to barrack and reach,
yet narcoleptic we, like Abram,
into a stone-forged pillow fall.

A farmer thirsts for a different spring,
digging beyond the blood-soaked dirt,
ever unslaked—
a gullet trust, a bellied destiny Easter belies.
Gunlets windbeaten by the hinter's dimming.
Abel's summons of blood surely taps
a fountain never failing.

To grow ever deeper and higher,
spying not the splaying order of root
or some leafs' mystic coding,
or the mass of stalk or ironed gates of bark,

but discerning the sap
in the furious flap of hummingbirds,
breath invisibly dipping
ever farther into the fountains of life—

A tiny pebble thrown toward the looming sunset is a poem
we write that skips toward the concentric hues of dawn,
vortices expanding melodies of horizons,
ours at auroral points of entry,
caresses propelling us further
into serving the scarred, not the scarring.

We get to wending
a universe, a garden,
a symphony awaits
We ourselves part bequeathe.

BIRTH OF TRAGEDY

Autumn maples, glowing wicks at dusk's extinguishing.

Or a volcanic text erupts to explode, sweeping the distance between peoples in their running

and melting their noise amidst a blizzard of soot

back into the crusts of earth.

Triliteral celebrity, idiot or genius,

what does your privilege say he is?

Walking into the glade the woodsman outlines grey bark,

tree handsome

Betrayed as he nears, lumbering gaits

overdetermined mastery of the backslung axe

Traps this scene in restlessness

centered in energies For her, tender and moist, inescapable

By his sere abrading skin, mirroring

As the thrush calls him back

Her gate calls him forth.

This will birth of tragedy

Where neither wine resolve nor abacus reveal.

VACATIONS FROM WRATHTOWN

Into the lot of Bashan's steepled beaker,
I roll to leaven with a Chevy's shofar's blare—
my palm kneading the steering wheel's center like to the toughest dough—
such chewy and acrid ambient,
bleating hegemony dressed in cool fine fibers,

That these beguiling toothy comportments may come crumbling down.
These bullet-flecked broadcasts of catastrophe become mirrors.

Statues cloaking phallus-grasped guns,
posturing imperturbable,
Rodin's Balzac, neighborhood-destroying.

For such members, this prepare:
How the seven-masted may trim its sail again to
bow the spear that howls and suckles steel!

Would rather snow's soft, still, silencing stores of variety's amplitude
paint these distempers with most hasty reverse:
I look around at my town new and old,
Sifting and cooling these unfamiliar kinds,
all swimming deep under the surface rage.

Householding schools far from the banks there,
flows destiny, ever to the quiet swells of its lyrics of exits followed and entrancings.

Camouflaged and unkeyed reCollect lathed to constancy's lure,
Histories of the death's lair—the beast's retrieval,
And the leisured bovine gibbets of resentment retooled
to rusticate clusters of cud and curd,

keening aromas sent of nature's hearth and grace's furnace
coruscating the tongue of our papers, our times—

To crunch through ear and eye arts' marrow,
Deep ingest for muscle and bone renewing than
Freezing reveries in Eden's ancient implants, our hearts now thawing
to climb down through stories of grey-scouring distemper
back to green,
seeking the sources of sensibility from which sprout
the remnant golden ruled, beloved.

SCOFFERS

Scoffers, always—*I know this,*
brooding from isolate rocks
at those who float along charmed waves,
sitting in the rump pew with albatross glances,
gauging furtively.

Their cackling—
as if some intervening serendipity will interview
others toward the same,
so to sup together in the suffocation of voids.

Brave harpies bravo brave chicks!
For the *virtuosity of contempt* ever suggests thee a new sunset:
"There's many a slip 'twixt that cup and that lip,"
they nod their redolent grave,
resonating with assurance that attempts
the quickest of exits—
even quicker than the expression,
"*You are wrong, sir,*"
with a penult's missing icing
the cake they try to bake of honor.

Their lumbering exit ever quickly begun,
such their craft: absence's art
lacking glamor's never ascending.

For the avoidant, hope is a mirror,
dear sisters—this I know.
Come back. Risk that rough-rocked lighting!
The table is set for you!

ROUTED TO LOGROÑO (JULY 2023)

Leaving orchard country gilded with pilfering reveries,
her muscle imaginings summoning oranges
illicitly gleaned from pre-suburban Edens.

We drive into the blue, guts lulled queasy
by the sinuous ascent punctuated and churned
by oncoming too-wides
careening over the divider seeking
momentary angular settlement for
centrifugally laden loads.

Vectors of narcotic commerce,
to feed and cushion a restaurant nation
under canopies of blaring Europop,
loop-mirroring the exhaust.

Breaking from tension,
among a cigarette butt-studded blacktop's
miniatures, a terracotta scheme,
smoke-hintered and enc(l)aved.

Monuments the mirrors to stubbed fingers,
nabbed mid-prison break from cancer's
ephemeral splay, these testify to denials
squeezing free from the rails of
rollercoastered and hasty fluck.

Our steps in this minefield are cobbled by disgust,
"Thank you for your service!" texturizing tears,
rapping the ears of every dying man
on every machine-scarred field.

But comes a tickling prayer, susurrating cool confidence
from a valley stream.

The triangles of grace bobbing our ears,
soothing and dousing these imaginings:
we come to know now this mountain cradle
by its abutment, its unpaved gurney.
Here the heart is traced as the heart shredded.

Grace's pointillism, its effluent dilutes
anxiety's chiaroscuro seep, as from collect's fissuring maw—
light bent by the weight of regrets. Ours.

Yet comes this refreshment to our own careening recollect:
pure and gentling scenery,
stitched by morning light tickling our squinting brows
as dialogue re-spooled on this mountain vineyard stage.

So to re-glyph our reel through this place,
to sense by engines and torches of encounter
the slightest torque, our loyalty to this genius of place—

through making—
and by aligning with—

sparking HistorY
never but partially, in fragments of irony or paradox revealed,
excerpt to human fragments of space-time:

Its ComedY,
the déjà vu *Kairesis* of eternity.

Disaggregate these our visions, and give i—
and by folk tunes accompanied by mountain runs,
we tremble into the next village,
toward the next dawn.

To induce another middle, plant another kiss,
these arrayed like sunflowers strobing past car windows—
their foliating orange-yellows matched by the whistles
of enduring breeze.

And so here that season's last leaf
falls into the earth's lap,
perhaps winter enduring,
to crackle under another cheek.

ENTERING TRAFFIC HOT

Entering traffic hot,

    my standards in this weaving lane

        plow to slam against life

            to combust heavenwards.

This my sc/huttle up the mountain

    to secure in flagging and leaden vapor—

Strife's ever blistering toil,

    transacting by the end-state's brain

        that plants deep this field,

            its bony and sere barrow.

By such vacation in a vacuum,

    a quantum prison's heliopause theology

        makes us dogs.

FREED BY THE POPPY'S EMBRACING WIND!

What conductor staved her atoms thus?

I become her sister, a Kestrel-wafted dandelion

of strobing float against blurred semaphores

of beetle-tactic limbs, soothing brows with only

what butterflies, brushing tendril lashed touches—

tangled and carved masks, as from acid blizzard turned.

Gilead calls us down, o mountain goats!

Plait and balm your paths into springs whence draw

the betrothed imprint and essence of destiny,

the green ambient posture of mirth and glow,

in pasture leaping from scoping mirroring trauma

of predatory and clouded epic,

now fermented into clapping fields attending

the chorus of apples and beeches.

Impressed by masted Giddyng-up,

nabbed in form and weather helm,

to ride its can(n)oning into an ever-cratering sun,

reshored in the junked eye ever broaching at the dawn,

to rudder its tread by griefs.

If the nights hold, we might scratch new stars to path us home,

rid of the melancholy of change that to excellencies

is hirsute Brutus becoming all in all.

And in the cradles of timeless event recurring,

find our grandsons not stepped, ginned, mouldering.

From my dream-sequined sleep I start,

urged by pen to what shook me,

sweet vase of psychoses seeking water, its womb—

reckonings of chaos dissolving responsibility.

Autumn, like flower petals, falls into my yellowed waking,

on which I set my breakfast.

I dig archives into the world

of absente heart,

O prophet O Tarkus bone of Lud,

In the chronicle of decline, the index dreg jigs,

while the world is repairing!

I hear by its ear an absence of music,

I spy through its eye an absence of heart,

all so that we might keep our shoes on at the unlocked heart,

to free our feet to self-bound eyes and ears directed.

Ovid and Goethe, sterile at the coming of Vulcan—

forged Notung will interrogate your ribs,

His temple of versified drive like no Freud,

that no Dali can frame.

There's a whiff of silicon here; better brine these walks

that caked your fences, their slats soothing,

alongside, but misleading by these, your troping treks.

Fruit emerges rather by shadow understories

where our stooping eye marries its arc to the ever-tipping sun

as spy the hanging winter apple:

the heart porous,

the drive and call to find, to struggle with the penning heart,

its river of electricity swimming, as its nose for refuge fills.

PERIPETETIC ACCOUNTS

Morning fog demon-deep,

dawn kneading the sun's

slink like across the

a wine drunk sea, spritzing the yard:

limbic and limb

occlude at my horizoning—

and others so unbedded.

The day will Fume and vibe its occasion,

thuddering rain across the oaks

while screen spitballs:

the Möbius exhaust of those ensnared.

Wondrous and passive-aggressive,

the middle finger!

"Malicious Compliance"—the riposte

of bearing, lawful deputies.

Such valorization by name

and abbeded as partisan

at the same time:

As servants of an animal state of nature—

what is such for man?—

soldiers are warriors who exult by killing

and who link its obsession

with honor's perverse preservations.

Ever trying, but inevitably failing,

to limn the line

between grace and violence,

to storehouse and dry ambition

the system of trade!

It's tricking a poe each day by

chrome and gold paints—

it thumbs a target, full throating,

hitching to:

Fasc-kinism Shrugs and Stabiles.

But a test unmapped

of us enter and exit

through the same stormy channel,

the same placenta—

ideas of both natured not yet tribed and cradled.

Wandering from what contests we

by leaving our tent

move forth to thoroughfare hide-bound tabernacles

—various ceilings—ram, goat, lamb—

and closet our role

in a temple's variegated costumery.

Where we go matters less than how we go,

and what we peer and pistil with

than any self-ifying Appropriation of Name.

GENIUS

When Era cuts

Stones of its epoch by a soft sword:

bent ecstasies follow,

limping heels bone their excavating marks,

among iced-shardings—

climinal pottery kilned,

forged by forget as strewn by fraught—

for what yokes the soil

shall caress the rootstock

To release green sap into what comes grafted for jibing breeze.

THURSDAY BEFORE CHRISTMAS, 2023

It's Thursday again, the day the leaf blowers pass through,
their high whine whittling like a penknife my ears
to round out the hastening by of weeks.
Their insistent noise from men to purchase a Saturday night beer—
I cannot begrudge (I know, I know), yet—

How can these weeks fast elapsing bring my unbalancing?
As hollowed out by noise's quick rush,
my vision is these ears' tunneling junction:
like weeks of leaf blowers, the cars' high beams at night rush,
warp my neck from the weave lanes.
Buoys proliferate like drying flowers dropped on caskets,
an allegory's condensation: "God is love," wrote the Old Revelator;
"Our God is a consuming fire," says the unnaming author.

And now I've burned the pancakes again.
The walnut flour shatters into sooty resentment mine.
I recoil from the stove like grease-scalded.

While new babies come in and the old exit,
the world's limb struggles to get out of gurneys,
to meet cohorts of striving possibles.
It's not the challenges of programming gadgetry as much as
to fresh smiles plaster
as friends move away, parents fade slow,
siblings claw the walls of addiction.

One more Thursday, then Christmas to grunt gunless through:
"Behold, he lies in his manger, Calling to himself Me and you . . ."
Joyfully my heart to leap and bread, singing as anew.

UPON LOOSING A TOOTH (A FIRST POEM FOR 2024)

Routines of an igneous beast *enslabs,*
Pulverizing, uplifting from spine burdened,
to swaddle gibbets or cradles,
swaying pendulous 'neath the nearwolves'
jutting cloud of teats.

Driving abutment of templed wind,
rousing the reshoring plow—
Two-edged masteries such billows,
throats exposed by tides like curtains.
Its moment in envy's destine:
As mercy journeys along with their slouching massage.

As so they wander
to mistaken rebirth by the mirror of history's steel,
and as they do,
they but mistake the meaning
for the slough and slink of insected lies'
amberfying,
mirror-encasing cruelties.

CALLING WATER

These ancient sleets stung mountain peaks,
Turning their crags into pillowed rumps
in which lovers repose, grind
to bubble forth.

Language, in cloudy cortex,
caged runoff re-iced
by distance northward flow—
a prior's—

Rooting the desert
in palms' tender embrace.

WHAT WAR IS THIS WITHOUT FOE?

What deeper tinctures come of Virgil's ho(m)e,
disguised as Dante's caduceus?

All war is against God,
and nature,
of neighbors who bring the scarcity
we blame.

The nature we share,
we blame for our death,
foreshadowing as youthful cages come s(h)oaring.

DOORING THE COURSE OF YOUTH

For youth hardening is the body's disposition,
while a philosopher's prism of sharded minds,
the doused memories which cuts the insipid duty to mirror witness,
its cheapening impulse behind every fetishizing of matter—
debts turned anodyne *"trespasses."*

As the latter type,
senility covers over errant maps from the echoing past into the body's germ,
clutching it firm and winking, wrinkling its mirror
as that most ardent and arduous hug on youth,
its poignant drum puncturing like a boot,
the mists married to ground and too soon slaking.

In compassion, *the Jubilee of age if found,*
the only decouple to the grave-bound drum solos,
manically epoxying the bones of futures, to statue there
as terror to its cement rooting pulse,
and morale nailed to wood.

Compassion's unalterable essence—
in the human mirror of the Creator's regard of his work
is the heart spread wide by memory's intentional, reverberating smudge

into nature palpable and crisp renewing,
kinesthetics tethering our heart to time and space,
anticipating its feasts that only arrive by inviting others.

With age the disproportion between the afflicted and the compassionate settles
into wheat's finest grinds.

Whence the fragility of age—musculature desiccate and febrile
while holding of possible carnality with penitence,
the beggar at my knee.

I by vision's ghost,
the countless times this left hand dug into my pant's pocket
for winning some gewgaw and ambered triviality.

And as *wither cries out to wither,*
the regent hand of hearts musters the reach's wallet-proxied aim.
I only ask you, old men who send rams of still moist tan
away to slay, to please God with their nostril whiffing death—
yours by their cousin-stretched pelts.

Is that nostril made of the integument that made peace
so to know the human flavor and odor of balm?
To love, father, and lay down walleting armies when the stink of the ape angel
comes surfing atop the mountain cooling gale?
Those noisome contentions, still and ever against God?

And at this knotted juncture,
when the will's account is ruptured by debits to sap:

Hölderlin's camel, clotted brigantines bearing,
broaching to suspend in the cool clean air
by grace's invisible tether and float alone,

where flaps the cliff-driving, like de'd Jeff Davis' ridden and tear-gnawed rag,
in unstopping, head lowering, back snapping salute to the prevalent—
until dry, twisted, and wrung
of its yacht-hungering blood bud-dying.

That we must attend to virtue's sweep,
to abandon all stratagems
and its realm ordering ethics
from pretender protectorates of clown lords,
that plant body cas(t)ings to compost renown and reputation.

But then to plow space and till place,
to green the earnest, the merry shoot, and mercy-ing effervescence,
opening to the eternal dooring of a neighbor wronged.

ARMS' THORN INTENDING EMBRACE

turned by her

simple smile, my leaf-line wish.

Such too for mine,

balming violence's stinging path.

And when they do such wonder,

fireworks me toward only You,

releasing from an encaved scribble

another counseling star.

And we, an astrolabed coil,

yoked for spring's Next grant and thrust.

F(L)ORWARD FROM FROWARD

I.

When I note dungarees
I expect she de-beds with the rooster
And flatbeds produce past pocket mansions
Cultivated like ornate cabbage on her matrimonial landstock,
Casting a gimlet eye to buffer its pang as she passes.

But what of I who with the owls?
Two species by tendrils volleying what cannot be seen

but only heard of the unknowing agencies in

darkest morning clocks?

Would you think this of me
Were I to pass, that in long cowled black,
its warp blazoning by a walking stick announced
as by cinematic wizard's length ignorance robing's conceit
perhapted with a fiddleheaded finial to crook the lost?

Nay-nooo: you'd think me woke by the noon in Walden,
The retreating kind. Not an owl shaking.

Which buckle to the detritus couture of failed ambitions, and find its moment:
Past dressed for success.
My wardrobe hangers of failed launch—

Deck shoes, Bermuda pants, yacht club belts, vented fishing wear
Button collar shirts (non-iron in the gamut shades of blue she hates),
Skinny jeans (most feathered by regret),

Kimono, fudged wingtips, last chance men's suits.
Polo pillories and alligators dripped like class honors.

Any of this I pick, a closet's lucky dipping
To trick that day's couture
Only serve to keep the elements from my skin
And scrutiny from my paunches.

II.

BUT,
If I am dressing for my current position in this, your idea of tragedy,

its position in space time, it's de rigueur—
Where I am fleeceheld,
With my quaint overlarge tenting by fluff of any kind,
Jacketing, sweatshirted, lining nylon work pants while skipping a few shaves
Make to look like I'm on my camping (soon to be accoutered a township criminal),

And I am, but not outdoors.

Rather, hoping for an invitation
To some social scene, where my jaunty is a mirror set in these dungarees
And I am bade to cozen and jean the host for a hearing:

III.

Though these may assure his order align, I simply but tear

a tent from abrading thorns
Wearing these lands as
My heart has set

the field's fecund soil restoring.

His tweed and pipe gin
the granddaddy's quail bounty,
Their stands invoked from a technic serf's inholding,
Long hatcheries before granddad fenced in
His crusading with determining' liege, banquets that

lay out terroir, an abbutting thousand-year claim, and geological.

Energies' conservation its farmer guide—

Not powers dissipating by pummel or harden
or forces wreck by displace crowding, or
the first fist of frost its conjuring

But that steppe breaking taiga of roots' occlude.

IV.

These lit as by angels coming—
Not as guardians of the winter's freeze,
But as *senders by a warming warning.*

Yet honor-captivated mind-ings
Stage human nature by scenes of bloody form,
Turning curses of failures into sips as cocktails report the front,
Their hymns of Agamemnon,
Those battles a venturer's bought town hall
gowned hatching bawl:

V.

Bringing curtains down
On potential—
Fodder married to a favored order turned and fenced by fields
Into continuant Flanders, staving off
repair
others' ripples so developing,
Ever seeking the rightful Romanov
To right ritual and bell Rome's third moo.

Such the vain
Appropriative of State—every state which

Sends soldiers but undiscipled in peace's arts, swaddling the elements
As Martin Lampe trailing his master
With The Umbrella precisely timed (a scion of mars, this lamp's

purpling flower for Herr Kant in veteran's service discipled by war?)
he most unthreatening sky shielding.

VI.

Neglecting assay save sortie and admiring incursion—
Every smallest invitation
by *experimerit to ball waltz into peacemaking,*
Even that most ennobled risk—calumny
In their inner circles.

The Prodigal Son a draftee in these, his enlisted to be enstied

Kept him mired in the regiment's house,
But it was *the recollection of the father's love*
Got him up to seek its home.

Against all Adam's nostalgia—all Abram's—
flaming swords angels guard against
The trap of worlds critically decayed, due date past,

As every elapsed generation hears *Qum lek!*

to get them up—

VII.

For the experience of *the turning God—*
us from our mountain strandings into mountain
ice melt watering valleys under Donner Pass
it enthalpic enlightening turn at the ritual snare of us blessing
Manners and plannings—

Such imposed and snail crawling deliberated on them as mirroring,
Inner circling, inner circling the drain
They themselves have put forth
As retrieve others by their fraught and decay-making of the dreaming
past.

VIII.

Simic demands of his
"poets worth reading usually [to] believe things

The age they live in no longer does.
Poets anachronistic, obsolete,
Unfashionable, and permanently contemporary."

Yeah, no. Poetricking hedge and system

Whirlpools away by trickerd thunderclouds,
inner circles to updraft by vestibule manners and conjurations

of floorboarded past imaginings (Isaiah 43:18).

Rather than investigatings
The ennobling of insighted Vectors-Of-Course
The current generation doesn't yet believe,
Yet growing out of—
As subject to interrogation,
The suborn clings that clawed before,
out of compost's sap into what is living, what surrounds us, grandly bowing.

As to enlighten the poetic, grandsired by Kant's recalcitrant student:
Who explores metaphysics accepts the duties of its metaphysics.
We measure out a measuring we ourselves are measured:
To torch a light from Christ brings that light to us to sense,
And to light cast from, to that itself casts upon,
The wave of observation that changes the eye
And makes it promontory, a friend and house.

To get as near to the current as possible,
To search deeply into its life from its spark,
The stream carrying its electricity in its swimming,
And so auscultate new things (Isa. 43:19–20) throbbing of its spirit,
By throbbing yours against its fire,
Feeling tales against your toes so you sway through a wilderness moment.

By our plathed knees as a salve or insistent scab,
Hone we in on its rejection until harmony of wave
Logics compelling awareness settles;

Its accountable plan and reckoning for daywear,
To move the epaulet from alligator and polo stick

And become a fish on a bicycle, petaling.

EX GLORIA HOMEOSTASI

To look around and see all the dispirited.
A mélange, a multiverse.
How majestic they'd look, uniformed and depositioned,
sifting the tentacling grime of fathers:
Sly Malebranche and Prometheus annealed
to thinking God's thoughts in retroject,
onto the elapse and nonsense terror,
which jabs its chrome frontispiece into ever-wandering circles,
home-ostatically brought to
oasis salutes to light-years,
dispensing of deep machine's dream:
the rub shoring this rictus,
yellowing, incised, grim and narcotic.

Begging for synchrony these louts,
to be knotted and branded by lightning,
and a good shave and kit and comb and blot
is all that is needed to buffer those
squinting: why at me?

Fall out, break order!
In rank is decay!
Phalanx ordered, this toad forged aloft without atlas or biscuit,
hospitaled by sing soil
and an iron-lunged notion of destiny
substituting for hope.

The fiddlehead's promise, from a nautilus' freedom express,
that some might taste its new necktar and shout,
beckoning others *to fallowed eureka,* to landings—
to hallow.

MOON AND STARS CLOUDED RELEASED

Moon and stars clouded, released,
wider of beam their dreaming masks cut from the infinite,
hemmed by leafy-floored forest cymbaled broom,
with crystal lips smacking with frost,
its susurrus buffering hoarse algo
and *snapping gutt(u/e)ral electronics of every (l)imitation speech.*

These beaming gems and pearled silence sport
through cochlear fibonacci,
like tickling caress from muffled moth sweep,
or sharks lateral atten[d]aeing deep underneath
the clowning salter of waves.

Their glistering sonar,
like webs sent from spiders
to sense what is ailing or hindered:
Food,
dangerous or beneficent,
everywhere around us.

In our confoundings now,
by meandering observations of popcorn science guiding,
desperately summoning God
by nature's probe,
its data reaching out to us in skin that cannot mirror
and antennae that do not love.

BOBCAT'S AURORA (MAY 11, 2024)

Pillars of praise roman candles from a wheezing sun.
So far south!
Such searchlights for heaven.

Northern Lights' orange strobed by bats,
Whiffling the night chill.
I have seen eclipses,
Never these.

But you lie silent and apart—
Who says hummingbirds never sleep?
Our place deepens
The nephesh of dawn,
Its moist emerald ember

Opens our lids to another's prowl.
As I emerge to find a big friendly of feline nature,

Like a piercing, this ebony beam flutes, burrows, and fettles my nostril:

His composting outside the door,
A bob-scat's night's passage hardening
As sun's brothering revive.

TO FIBER GALAXIES

To galaxy filament
sequined by strange esurience.
I shudder.

Or *Lazarus woken from death with a single tear.*
More still should negligent and naught I shudder.

But God is not I.
Joy will come, baby Achilles true.
By songs cut your spears out from inherited schemes
And *circumcise the heavens by which obscuring lights you tread.*

Singing grace carves its echo from silent snowdrop,

And God's pupils ripple time.

ANALOGIA ENTRANCE

Antic Entis entrances
Rodeo Beach's yestered noon prophetic,
Where muse of water and wind unbuckled birthing
Angles of riptide, swells as feminine as the white wash drags
Our blinks back the deep toward another layering heliopause:

As zippers emerge from these vortices
Of back-and-forth waving,
Sometimes two ways along the same seam at once,
Small geysers at their collision.
These zippers effervesce—I wrote this once to charm you—
Trailing like a shark honing prey.

High rock outcroppings
Individuate, snails of drifting magma.
The north beach end:
Sailing, cushioning, green shoots and guano blots,
As by a paintbrush splayed to sway
With the horizon's Colossus.

A broad prow, these rocks
Jut and pulverize our swells' returns,
Exploding in splinters of white sun,
Sharding the surf with mirroring hoar's glinterings.

I suckled near Lake Michigan dunes
And swaddled by mid-Atlantic shores.
Still, the waves on northern California beaches crash into
My enchantments like no other.

Sun and wind embracing the west conduct its surf by:
Rolling booms, punctuating to the background susurrus
Of fizzing foam and sand skitterings,
Feasting like gnats on the shin of this

Harb(r)inger—this thalassal theater and tan,
Fabric saddling, bronco sublime,
For me, heaven's vagina.

VII.

Back Down Modern
When by tent or text leads the Sun

Jacob's Ladder of elegy and lament—up and down through grief, satire, political witness, and metaphysical critique, toward redemptive inquiries.

ORBITUARIES

More than anyone, *poetry needs frankenSt(r)aining,* a diagnosis.
His gravestone has left a trail of incomprehension
And backchannel gossip of torqued avoidance
Since his face first took up the ear, a ram's mess unlikely to tidy.

His soul T(o)uring—a journey's testing—
I found myself ensnared: *his st(r)ain—both!—*
Yet unnamed becomes of mine!

Was it ever so?
In qua-trained sequencing fury's vatic coriolis rearranged
To give another hope, another umbilicus and din
To nation, place, and escape Nemesis?

But I'm tanned now, in a Ten[t]way woke,
Shoulders torqued from scoffing, mine theirs,
Pelted by his obscurities on the switchbacks to this sulcus,
Such jags coughed by an eden's alien magma.

Doctor, bring me—this too—
Back to the well-marked comradery of sapience unobliging!
For I bereft and unarmed from cajolery and laughing
Am bars now to sweet compellence' gardens,

But only in the grim and repairing lashed,
Of resistance's heart-swell eternals.
Inside language trapping,
Always to earth and from earth,
This eden privileging hymning of earth.

AS THE DEER

As the deer to the sparking stream hooves her rush,
So my thirst stakes their trails decomposing,
Stoked by a spinal autobahn's late overlay—
Careerist *aspict*—its vision unjolted and congealing,
Haste-slaked lava for Etna's wine-ambering cup.

My fingers chisel for this hollowing bone,
Prying apart the reeds of your back and shoulders,
As the music jackhammers, excavates its hustles *kneed.*

Into the first carriage lane probing, then deeper,
To the stilting heels of heavy-bosomed planters two-stepping
Seed into furrows,
Windsnapping fields into a neighbor's map,
Hybridizing unhusked amity.

Then to these dear, *my deer.*
In such other moments we pranced these stilts
As to sip from whist atop those canyoning things
That box by *antlering rhythme,*
And give scent to the elbows of lust surrounding,
Like acrid ozone, the tickle of humbug.

Our twitch and clutch of prophecy resuming,
Denying, anticipating each harmonic commentary,
Of jig-addling sackbutters,
Frontmen implicating our limbs and grasp
In his finger *castworks,* bifocaling
Every smooth-jeaned booty
Flexing outside of the mirror's *g(l)aze.*

That nature is the sun setting among these reeds
For some a wick never spirited,
So whiskered, our sweat now whisped by tears,
Where bean fields whistle through with orphaning bitters
Left mossed and waft
By arid bop abandon to

Scrub the pins and hazened ear of fauns by deafness now
Emfossiled by oil smoking john,
Deere scarifying the breeze with coughing,
Unbraiding in its circling,
The square and guzzle ghosting reel.

UMBRELLAS

Umbrellas these ever cocked,
Drip panning the armchairs of Titans,
And besides fireside lamps poised to quill and puncture clouds,
Loosing brigand Prometheus, darkening furies
As *Hermes bring-wing about.*
In shadow then is the Overarch!

The Anarch beyond all language
And prior to all gods
Save Nemesis!—for such yet babooning, hail is seeded
To ever braid the yorn fire,
And reshadow such warrant that
Propped Aristocles' stains
And cushions Schelling's yet-now prelates
In alarm at these circlets' 'clipse enduring.

Only now comes the wailing horning gaols of recall's chisel,
As miswrite poets hermit from the clime of history
We but mistake for grace's absentinth.

So we brand our own absolute of absence as *cocksure,*
Brandishing like kamikaze kisses
Our *cha cha portraits of history.*

While honey-shaping flowers are as glazing mirror's tingle in our vision,
Twitching prophecies salient and moistened,
As *dew-ligatured melody* surely to those *umbrellad piercings,*
By peacemaking doubtless restore.

BACK IT UP

My garage shop, *the Tinkery,*
And my armchair fireplace, *the Thinkery.*

Let us peer in with infinite monkeys,
contained by eternity's typewriter and long farewell,
to collect the repeating works of Shakespeare,
and honey them a question,
to suck a thumb posing:

Will a finite number of silicon boxes,
o browed and templing—may it—
processing fossils and lab patterns,
ever get Satan out of hell?

Beauty aligns with striving for duration but smiles with change:

My garage shop, *the Tinkery,*
And my fireplaced armchair, *the Thinkery.*

OUTPOSTED MODERN

—widening surrounds becoming aware and eterne, we attend,
Every individual g(r)asping at energies, the cosmic, perichoretic,
And obliged we jamb, most punchdrunk by turnedly, readily, and re-
sponding, inviting.

Industrial *uni-form-ing* perches now *birdsprung*,
And so, and do,
By curtsies to music unboxed to sap into space
And garden them into place,
So alert a rhythm, charmed fury against future's strait.
The whole's knee *stich-ing*, limbs *antici-pate-ing*
A realm *resonant*,
Un(g)loving the pugilistic,
Membering right arm's shield now into a guided waist's cradle,
And the spear's left arm, our *re-membering axis from thrown*
Of legend to girdle.

Never hardened heaven-ward,
But wobble out new stars by these arm arrows pointing,
Plastic rotating we give them muscle tensed like whiskers
To understory what has boxed and cuffed to the very source,
Which the boxings can untree in itself and live and leaf again.

The ramifying sip
Rooting freshets that ever unbox the priors,
Which is the rebirth for *novum*, for repair of
Nero's poor gastrulating bow and from error's weeding Pharaoh—
A tuning fork then put away, to restory growth of fresh, greening song.

Like sonatas, codas like ferns carrying multitudes—
Fiddleheaded teleologies begun retrograde,

Crashing against its axis and retorqued for an oceanic vectoring potent
And summary plunk of a string, like a Mahlerian,
Its contenting final *heartgasp,* which is—

FATHERHOOD

Life spent
escaping the shadow that seedlinged us.
Instead,
to bequeath our derooting, through shade rerouting's escape
into legacy's sun efflorescing limbs.

The father of time
creates seasonings of challenge and hybrid grace
To shape us fatherhoods of timebearing children,
as motherhoods of children-bearing time.

Dutifully I try to teach him of realism:
"Shampoo artists shape all, rinse vectors the repeat!"
That every weighing of evil and choosing the lesser

Frankensteins us better maths.

And he pushes back with ideal's certainties
for unalloyed good for some unallowed. He sings:

"Each moment is by God created
to inspire and breathe an enduring legacy

from shaping our moment."

"Our virtues alone makes our Planning.

And only for peacemaking we plan."

I smile.
He bears the sunrise.

AMERICAN PASTORAL

My boy Clark,

six softshells in the glove box,

an iced bushel, oysters in the trunk,

leaving Maryland,

and headed home.

Pack of smokes,

tall boys,

and Depends in the back seat

'cause mortality wheezes its holy breath

through tide and traffic, and

it's a long damn drive.

RECOLLECTION

To pause *ankling*, boys,
Up from such antlering cheek and booze,
And compass Christ's
eterne becoming—
Seen first Romping, vulpine in green gold grass-scaped toothy,
To then glassing by their bubbles of memory
The Shimmerings of joyous regret!

So avast—such now alone I seek to mete.
Others may me for inquest lie,
Even to hiss my brow by sand
Turtled from monks—
And crack me open like a coconut seeking a sweet juice,
Through its ear's effervescence tinge and linger—
By which His oasis stakes its palm
To a muscle-helming tongue and trimmed and homing sail.

ELECTION DAY EVE ABSTRACTION 2024

The *Dupth* and *Webth* of blacklight couture
Seen as yellow incisors rip wholes,
Sundering green expectations
By barking binaries
D(r)ecked out with prophecy and compelling,
Raising the smithereen sweats of trepidation
That salt the glower and forge partisan's brow,
But flare as a phosphorus pulse
To grab the night by the throat of lies,

A des(ic)canting and curtaining choir—
The crumbling and smearing of the erstwhile,
Abrading our ear that honeyed its hopes now pirating.

You know surely—
I'm surprised you don't—
How buildings clubbed your unique sense
To tempo a pattern, ours to predict and set toward arson.

Yet mistake never these flues and familiars for the certain—
This though but birthlings expect!
As what is heavy-booted by these trampings
Dig into souls,
A well's deep gushing,
Their flows twist inward
The shoveled palms of mountains graded for ramparts,
To enclose their flowered paths for supplication,
Not aloft clutching into ever more shadow sufficants,
The mind vaginations unmeriting and moated grey,

But assembling their points to lush and verdant stories—
Of those friendly and saga-salted wise from enduring,
Braiding destiny by the rocks' deepest skittered heart,
Broaching midst valley-intricating streams.

VIII.

Unbunkering

Wrestling culture's disinheriting secular exhaustion, metaphysical dislocation, and poetic degeneration.

THE ROUSTINGS

Child, we were born into this promise,
Where nothing stings more than selling out to the lesser evil,
And discovering no one except the purchasing agents of the greater obscene observe—
For there is a glut, but a gut to stuff.

Bereft then of deliveries and takings,
We stand hugging our shoulders in a barren marketplace,
Rocking like abandoned puppies in a cage,
Holding nothing of vendible value in a machine-cranked age,
Artisans only of skulls, fantasies, vengeance.

These, like bony grasps, the undercarriage of order no one thrives upon,
Lusts for, we are emptied elites of the wasp's false phallus—
Until the pus shudders in us,
Its dark energies downshift,
Wending us like wafts of whisper from the unhearted belly's growling
Toward the creaking abundance of the heart's laden table,
Companions laced into nature's soi/ul herself
And scoured by us its contour of turning's age, this.

>   The Spirit enflames—it does not calcify, nor eggshatter cling, nor ascend from ashes' nest—

>   The Logos invites, faith appropriates, but neither orders or chains to sculpt or fossil—

The emerging awareness is storied inlay, whispered and unpriced,
A machined forc/ge,
Itself-asserted name to cavity a name where a heart was absent . . .
Worthy of accomplice only to sclerosis of grace,

Which finds its most pointed challenge, dynamiting the joust
To astonish and overwhelm as it pushes in, expands, unclots, and claims these sinews.

For all that rises must descend, pop silently,
To litter the limits of arrogance, heroism's geomancy, feeding the pistil—
The phenology of the pusillanimous, metaphysic even when the most expected recurs!

This enchantment is shattering—as all vanguard details—
And of its harbingers inside this little corner of the creation,
We inhale as contemplative inebriates with Her metaphors brimming over,
Without cost but unsating,
Making ours the aroma of eternity,
Its heart-quickening sublime feeding the pulse
By which we drum out our meaning
And bake into its energies frostflakes,
Enduring to the eye but smeared by the touch.

So we do abide,
Hymning gratitude, contentment, joy, welcome,
Because we cultivated the measure and sendings of promise.

THE RISK OF FALLING

Hip-fracturing risk increasing
Ages its visual field,
From backshadowing slopes the big future better
Than every else routing—
Presuming to understand shadow first off
And act after—

But now,
To steady oneself by the very ground,
Forwarding the very nearby and now,
Only stopping,
Completely still,
To scope the medium itself—
Now changed by age's decrepitude,
Presuming nevermore to eagled-spread soar by mind,
Like never looking to the plane strut in turbulence
But to the squeaking bulkhead's semaphore to unquease.

And only then, so very occasionally,
Coming to a complete moment abed,
To contemplate—prone—what is soaring ever higher,
Actually what is outside oneself's halting.

What is not actually accompanying oneself,
But those petty concerns about dignity, now dimming—
About staking mountains to claw by one's youth,
About cramponing with infinities;
Not to lend aid and service by insight,
But to grab the collar of heaven,
To state your grievance, allowance—
To justify resentment and its bone with envy

By one's self-necessity to exist as the dawn,
And by that unaccountably and selfishly, prismatically,
dress it in the dead skins of favored order.

But now I am aged,
Unbalanced but not unbalancing,
Idiosyncratic but not esoteric,
Crepuscular—
Moving the lab smells of pillage square
Into the peopled environs where
Grace to me stinks when sometimes enemies afford it,
And at others is aromatic with blessing and memory.

A glimpse of the medium that beckoned you to impress,
To own its form and
Conscript the future its semblance as your claim to know beauty.

But now, from ankle heights savored for its you-ness alone—
That you-ness that is loved and ramifies, for its you-sake,
Not its future-sake,
But its neighbor-scape, see sawing to take wing.

EVANGELISM

Ever the stone guest, insipid phaiph,
Tesseracting a promise
By maps of escaping
Or of its settled concourse aligning the generative,
Soundtracking summons against the crossroads of dusk,
As perichoresis entrancing.

A pistil of dandelionizing
Or a pestle for pulvic statuary
Capping chaos' aquifer?

How may I thee lure
To take time's chisel
And score its wrist onto mausoleuming histories,
Clawing out olives from the precipitate jerk and shuffle of tanks,
Pressing out its grey matter—
The tribunes of *ego gurgitans,*
Their stanchings staked to salute
A state(d) human form as nature's harmony?

By the heart's ear perceiving,
Rewater our brow's eye renewing,
To spy we sun's pillaring runway, as

Poetry climbs down:
Its prisming promises against prisoning's engraven burials—

Eloquence is a sabbath from society's *amour propre.*

Instead to folkwalk children
Through this ebbing fo(u)rth night's smear

And learn new songs
Of dawn's only truth and spear.

MUDDY CHANNEL RUNOFF INTO BAY (12242024)

Zone of mixing kicking up a horse's mane
And ever gasping, nose lashed fleck—by
Who's below, ever swept?

A highway drives me north,
under intermittent drizzle and shifting clouds
Reveal understories of a rainbow struggling
To defragment and give birth to wholeness.

Each shifting cloud, by wind above my seat,
Reveals new partial panes, arcs ebbing, joining, dissolving,
Each wiper moment like a thumb leafing
Through a text of sky.

This fingered sunlit wind: can it,
Will it reveal its full horizon?
Can yet, never yet—the Christmas Eve.

Is this rodomontade of metaphor
nature's relentingless messaging—
Our gods ever shuffled by Spirit
In moments to arrive by history's rest?

CALENDARS' MIDNIGHT ELIDING

Ungated rafters of pulsing sweat,
this pergola at New Year's, its Eve a
broad and sequined chassis that backs into my Orphic lane:

What plucked out a dusty Terpsichord,
dumb lucked and thumb bare tune,

its joinery a hatnail to echoing,
the harness its strange curtsey, butt up, pelvis planked and mantled,
eyes avoiding (there are different gravities working)
to cast toward pole's fishing?

What Hölderlin guides this underworld to her Arendt
by light-flecked, torch-cozening moons,
disco-orbed archaeologies machined in chrome?

Goethe here lies in staining perches of pomegranate,
a penumbra of Purgatory ever dragnetted and peeled by youth,
angling for Proserpina's course, yet themselves pulled off course and deep
like Tannhauser and Faust, to converge—
narcotized by eros' promised Lethes but wasped and broaching,
a chairlubber fate now recruiting.

While wolves circle about her in the corn, does she ask:

of her lecterned lover over there in thinkentein's groove most abysmal un-naming,
aware only of energies unleashed not created but surely destroyed,
tormented by wordless time,
The lowing of the lowest amplified as

cows uddering their bells by fourthings?
Far more telluric and discordant than disco:
How insipid its contrapasso's harpy teet,
its drip drip milk she-etching metals of reproach!

Now return, timed position, as it grabs to lift not throws to redust:
you smirk, is it a leer?—*you have no idea*—
striving inscrutably but siren clear.
But I remember those cowbells and restrain,
like a boxer before a championship match.

Will come our (with)draw as the ever uncommon years close book
while second hand's trident gigs water and light where it coruscates and bounces:
gravity's compel claws at entropy's alluring,
its heaven-hooking enclosure.

These gleamings not by toothy grins greased by dripping brows
but through a mouth that opens in greeting
by simply turning its ear around
to cast a buoy of embrace,
surfacing us both in sonambula's vertical horizoning
toward a changed Sonrisa.

LIGHT WHICH A SILENCE LEARNS HER CRAFT

This onanist lifts mirrored knees lingering too long,
its freezing substance outstretched palms
like mountains advanced against changing shadow,
its horizons in legs that knew no ram's craft,
instead,
that a Holy monast would rule his piety,
bring a saint's heart by company.

In silence alone was recipe of purpose floured,
nothingness leavened by quaking to venturing,
taking awe by hand, learning
to bake—
with the tools' purloined apprentice to curiosity's armchair
and the oven of grandmothering
nourishing the joints of young moveries.

Field Blentings arrive by diligence' wine,
sustaining through time reflecting what sustains by time—
to leaven seasons by ami(d)sting elements—
animals sailing their pelts and repass't candling—
to wheatcake pews with dollops of grace:
Enswaling manna, renewing the embrous f(el)lows,
never dousing, never doused.

The Attributing All comes by such crafting.
And by this All moment reach we toward greater alls,
by weaving shuttles outward may we toward only middle make:
A carpet is heavenly hanging's past effort,
ours to needlepoint our fill, slowing
as other thumbs stray their eyes near.

The Aligned and Attendant—*in every all*—comes beauty from the middle.
Waves of bucksparkle, unshaped and unshaping,
the complete and compel,
for to what is still untouched
and into the warmth that is
both flicker and moment,
like a shed feather, cheek pinion scraping,
a caressed memory that is the fingers' gushing—

Light.
In which silence learns its craft.
Light where silence takes to dance.

SHIP OF STATE, SHIP OF FOOLS

Citizen of the state
of nature in futility, the thro(w)ne of anxiousness,
where I cannot see you because of chains yours and mine
which have us rowing on different decks—
on what ride hope of a sea, though I cannot see,
toward a land known in its nagging hill's vaguery?

What are your rations? *I cannot but ask.*
How cushioned and by What sergeant drums?

A discipline, it seems we make to now row, to space

and new gods find, to channel their
cauldron sere by technics of glaciers we have already in memory's
smudging world?
Will sleep allow, or its nights
pecked as meals by worms of reproach?

All so the emperor can find another justice,
and dream of another heaven,
and rub the cream of children's tears on the welts mirrored in him.

And leave the fetch of home for a dim song and color of our seas
for the jolt of reordered moonlights,

to find an escape from entropies certained by muddied holes,
our hoarding musked fire,
and scratch our fingers in its embrace,
to bed a sand-banquet ziggurat in words that loose of duty to you?

TREE OF LIFE

Can I sense the glide of light through your hair—*am I not supposed to*—
The gladness bubbling, your fingertipped massage
into its grey and rooting vegetable path
whence goats come tumbling their strife from high places
toward the browed promontories eroded from youth
by smooth and sweetening riverstone?

Can I see we grafted to olives, both born by nature,
then torn off by our wildings—*now we two both wild,*
grafted into a house(h)oldening's vine,
trunking its b/holster with the b/harks of age?

Can I find our surface, and by what is for us this—
a gardenyard for courting,
where fronds of palms tune the breeze that rustles your maiden—
does it sing, does it (g)rasp—
where she drew me a bucket washing and leasehold?

Can I unfurl your fiddlehead flagging pain
that looped ever tightly coiled but launched,
a greening as nautic service toward unending?

Was I too such—is ours such blaring, cantoring step?
You hide our grasp and twitches by eyelids clenching,
its mortar against scrutiny,
torched by the celery crunch and boot broach of oak by our waltz.

Only by this orange respite from sight can you feel me planting music
into you,
as you muscle assent to its ancestor and skeleton energies,
its heeling caligraphy.

How can your hair be a goatherd, a bleating stream and so such of beauty?
No: it is not by lookward orange but the greenward journeying—
its unknotting and net-letting,
its unslitting greensward to well-watering plains and tabernacles dawning:

Where pain is ever marked but no longer pelts
and your hair waterfalls that splash my lips like a slap its feathered guide.

These run to over the cobbles and seed of time once oiling by,
pestled now twining by the pull of sunlight,
and friending and swelling by the swim saps of our own make,
legible only to who cross and us bridge.

MOONSHONE EARTH (01122025)

It was wax January supposed, gibbous not gibbet,
this sabbath night on the even of the year's full first light.

Near midnight after us,
I went out to breathe the glistening grey radiance,
where every tree's bark was as birch,
papery and feathery, as if trembling with that shine.

And the grass—tiny snails its host afar—
surely merged as currents, small ripples of this night surface,
chambers soundless these to mix

By this dark torching tremble
and dim shimmer.

This hoar, winter crisp striving,
now thumped with warmer breeze the cluster
fragrant and moist.

Though a shadow, its subjects,
evade by damming energies—
that deed through our coursing
and endures, staving music
by that moon centrifugal,

most tidally momentous, the most stately dervish spiral
tonight Straight Overhead pouring into time
its mix of closed positioning and energy's
ever pray replenishing.

And I am by bile and humours—yours and mine—intricated

not in luminaries' determination but as statuary

in conservation of energy

> creations like the signal cycles of its nature
> married to ours,
> history and biography perspecting and panning the surround
> for something ungoldening in that prospect—that prospect of

Law's

> *always surprised, but never shocked by*

conservation of the source, its wonder.

Tonight's mirroring moon came glimning
fervescent—the sparkle of daylight
to shift and bridge into the sundown.

A new year shaping like palms pressing my waist,
such my own travel, now yours,
as we look and await even its lupine circles.

And the moonshone God wakes to.

MILLWORKING ADUMBRATION

Except by this, my clowning prophet

to suborn Lavatch's bard and master,

His but declare of forms,

Lexicon's canon shots, aimed

by lectionaries of shouldering Titans,

Such predications of step-down,

to logic winnow Theses to birth-throttle later Theses,

and from its clutch of young Theses

shut the door to new theses

as determined determined

determining to thresh a threshold thereby,

to regarb history's nominals

in Pantegruel's clowning absolutes

that are but entropy's priestly robes

As shell with eternity come forlain with weight and rigidities atop one's soul,

but to crack its gate is to soar by language nonetheless.

And skeletons fixing bony fingers

at sin and decline

but as to only cultural manners waning

themselves they harbinger.

So the moth circles on,

our blazes lit for its little riddings,

such comforting our discomforts and

With a glass a-port and a good fire,

and the victrola splaying Brahms onto

an armchair hosting Gibbon's

hanging moon service,

and cigar to lamp and ember for at least a night,

though the window peers at

a calm and sparkling sky and grass,

against the cries and howls

against seasons that lash our brow

And as we finally a-bed his logic,

perhaps to a-wake with knighted scribbles to Logos

when we've finally unbent our knee

and get up and move,

For every Plato'd finger extending toward eternal light to carve out

a form turns Gangrene, and spreads contagion's Nemesis.

So to overarch its switch and bridge

by hard and necessary effort to eyebrow and kin the palm by opening to

change in every arriving possible, by every re-birth.

SHEPHERD'S PIPE

Besotted with myth and tact mercurial,
the georgic master's professionless youth
made idylls of the shepherd's song
to the beauty of surpassing,
so to bridge with sponsor;

how emboldened becomes his play
for the wagers of nations,
sourced in the ruddy Rubicon
of divine undertaker Julius
with the muddy knobs of Latin,

and the math-ing out of ends,
driving generals into labyrinths of mind
and ending in a coin flip,

instead for his adopted nephew,
in the split and stabbed breast
of petitionary Turnus . . .
and CUT, throwing its denarius saved now to us.

The state poet's disenchantment
with this *cut-craft and bullnationing*
bids to venture over the lip of mind's labyrinth
into an abyss, to find—
like John of the Cross—
what rises that enraged and bloody beast.

This poet, now by his laters made general,
breathes out a new craft
to loft a third Rome's marble grey-streaking candle.

Or Dali, ceiling his chamber
with grotesque Sistinery,
as Solsticery, the feet of lurid painted titans pressing down
where an outstretched finger beckons and gifts—
rebuking by that finger his coiffed art of stomping.

That we are hated until we fashion our ownedness.

Or to have the comfort of Dante,
to name his rivals burning in agony
for eternity in hell.
To name names!
And their hellscape recursives!

All these define worlds as substances—
sent as paper mausoleums
for the charnel of its colonized children,
such graven, its skill and terrible knowledge.

Virgil's deathbed—
his instruction to sundown the estranging source,
the West and its wolfening nature,
by language intricated in all these!
Ceres magna est de abolenda Aeneide.

To the shepherd's song allow
to pierce a patron's dark night howling by,
trodding instead unshod—unshoeing to nomad a new home—

shoonshining, Abrahamic,
repenting of those mounds of pilfer and shoes,
haunting at the Holocaust Museum—

not with a founding murder justified
and then shadow amassing and building,
but with one re-occasioned by petitionary sacrifice.

And come tents to board
upon galleys to embark,
like the shipwrecked apostle,
not as a storm blowing its haven tomorrows,

but with a prayer to the sea's remaking.

To rise up from civilization is daily

to be bested by choice: the fining spirit and declining ash,

of nemesis and eros as the fire gastrulation of Phoenix grey feather—

Its sizzle to come in fierce—geodesic scaldings de-wombing algorithmic hijack of reality.

Thence to begin its faring,
with *"Call me Elroy"* to fish, not slay monsters.

Travels by grain and amphorae-stuffed holds,
abundance—
Sustaining, calling to Himself me and you.

Where the Markan witness
cuts to silence, anothering hope
that passes even unto beds arresting.

Where the poet who opened an underworld
per sortes Vergilianae—
some even now still play,
holy dipping in a scripture of ambition.

But this bed, given the choice
of a well-loved path, enduring—
rather than one final cast or wink—

For he has been embraced
for his Youth and Repentant Debt to Dying,
as the dove dips into final awareness flashing.

For in the shepherd's pipe
is a heart that beats with healing grace,
and for which is our well-pleased burden—
to mete and peal every waking day
toward healing moments,
craft-readying, and re-viewed.

BLESSED TO ESCAPE

the sordid and empty events
of army barkers carnivaling and voracious,

my body was instead
tabernacled by
its observatory middle time in Christ,

in a thor-pageanted hammer
of resonating,
resisting,
conciliating,

that tested my spirit
to His unfolding call.

Now,
Climinal as Lexemic Luther
and priest of trembling revelations,

I set—
an Archivist of the
busting forth
not in tongues
but in bursting images,

the Oracular machining of dead memory
into the kindred collects
of expression
with no sunsets.

Constituted stenographer
for the forgetting god of our fantasies,

I startled
into choirmastering dissonated elevations,

from a pre-carnate river
to ligature of late baptism,

and the vectoring cleansing
of speech by babble-smashing B(aal)S.

IX.

Tracking Energies' After Imaging

Poiesis blasts into form, dogma, and syntax toward transfiguration; Unshrowding the apocalyptic and perceptual by inner recourse of *eros* and *agape*; Navigating the cosmos by new stars and instruments.

ANTHROPROLOGOS

Whiffing mix of lantern kerosene and silicon,
ignited moths braid peril flimsy, spins
inject's eaten space—
across our track of armchair cushions
and dinner jackets.

Technologos promises simple represents—
production resets of clay models sprung and trunkless,
severed from history
by truncates of hegemons.

The truth about nature—much less reality
cannot be stated as principle or ground

for more reduction, like sauce,
but must be troweled in full—
lest our changed means
means our change.

GRACESCAPE/ING

(for whom a gibbeting moon casts shadows).

desire Unboxed
and put into the sieves of body memory clutching,
its muscles jigging to lure words these,
and put forth that struggling to forth more—

These words of a life rerouted and rehearted,
leaving the vain pursuit to hottub in the Mind Infinite:

My words seeking to rise like bubbles from this deep,
those which witness to divers prior's sleep.

And now those at surface seek from the keep a face,
making me wonder—noises of ambient outer space
are ever accessible to our machine coursing rhymes,
because it is poetry and not mathed sublimes.

The energy of eternity's embodying climb
may only find number as grace's-aligned prime.

So who can know whether static is quantum sizzle,
or the rain parting ways with her daughter, drizzle?

A wind that exceeds its grasp is but a heart denuding or a shoulder unrolling.

Or a dead star holding to us patiently on
until the whole comes entaphed by our working, anon?

Thus scapegraces repaired by gastrulations
for Spirit making *gracescape, congratulations.*

For allows nothing a mime to emulate
eterne words, unarrowing time, sun's radiate.

We come potentiate for poetentate time bornings
and no longer anticipate unend's forlornings.

Thus may truth only serve hopes,
no longer death within its tropes.

And same such prose which lingers as critics,
of forces imposing entropic enclitics.

But the poem dances, indestructable light

And by virtue of Him has left the fight.

ANATOMY'S UNBUCKLING

Every couture of self-creation is birthed in failure,
so especially regendering tries on Sarai's spirit,
pulling against barren closets to
transfigure nature by dress—a shadow of desire giving rise to gen(i)us as artefactant.

But rather than to particulars reduced,
not as potentate comes

but to potentiate essence

that keys the locked nature's gift personal and extensible.
Such is made vague by the key's investigate facet,
except in our better dreams—
of Peter, Andrew, and John behind a rock
learning that Moses, Elijah, and Jesus shine for their sight and hides.

A hollow insist on anatomy
plants its security and comfort,
like all losing, in plantations of flags and draperies.

The mature labor to plant arms, and deepest at that,
awaying sculpting ground by chiseling marmoreal shadows,
toward softer seas and crafts of care—
eroding magma and mountain by sunshine's steady drops.

Orders of magnitude the energy to turnbuckle
quanta of genius whims emerging—

even intricating the merest molecule, everywhere pulsing with time.
How much less to tether an arriving world?

But it is impossible—*mortal lock negated*—
to stake certainty in the shafts of dead ancestries,
the backshadowing of entropy as closure.

The geometry of mercy bends time without vertigo or boxing,

seeding renewal not repeat.

At best, our archives bear witness

to faculties of the sundowning,

to morrowing our households,

and to why we could now speak, and in part,

how our children might find the light and breeze for the difficult, necessary changes to

the monk's enclosure ideals at the night,
instead in blessed usufruct to hoe coming dawn.

So by living
we to sate atop a sled of warm corn but down its slope,
novelties of history and nature popping out at us—
not as movie miracles,
but under a day's changing sun.

Light understories with the season's pollen,
revealing justice *we mistake for grim shadow*
pecks at our vision as the new day's growth of berries on vines.

By aligning and enduring, indestructible, such
to portion and account

Creation's *will, alone absolute*, its dispense—
yet on earth placed to evolve by forms:
its mirroring,
by stitching the inside fabrics of eye and ear, and reweaving—
as sup our delights,

As stitches the cosmos by threads of divine intention, we needles fingers
find and heart attaching
to source each moment anew.

Not retrieving sepia that sepiates,

but new patches by our key and chromatic merits as well.

For as the phallus withers, beauty fades,

but the energizing Word endures.

VIRGINS' HEAVEN REJOICE

How in the age of thinking machines,

breaking forth oligarchs' ends,

can we fail enter the decadence of human nature?

And come down to flourish with what we've put by,

this garment we've woven at our earthiness—

in a birth's explosiveness, pulling roots from the sun by destined thorns,

planished gimcracks now by ear and eye lathed, auscultating human

essence by its ejaculate joy and blood?

At those times where mind separates from heart,

as philosophers poets,

is decadence from bunkers of war spied or (imp)lied,

or when hearts' command, concupiscent ambition through parted curtains torn?

By which is signal reconciled love—

as the Steppenwolf seeks,

by the nightclub intrigues waking nightmares

by two-steps, moving from

agriculture and courtship

to praise, Tissue B'Av's maidening quiver not by grit or design

but by throughways and coursing, seeking landings:

So as Solomon learns

that virginities we regain,

restitched in material loving indeed!

AURA ABOUTING 12262024

Today is our un-Boxing day,
which from now on is a dancing day.
Pugilism's posture inverting:

Switch out your spear's raising,
your partner's arm now lifting
by Her lead and hand,
and drop your shield unwonted
to cradle her waist, to you press her gently.

And as your heels foursoming ventures unsquaring,
they trowel for where provident seeds find root.

Perichoresis eternally (s)plays its
intending
flowering by us today.

IMAGINE SURVEYING LIKE GOETHE

Imagine surveying like Goethe
from the most high-mountained conceit
and asking of a sundown, a dawn,
a green gold field wave of wheat, its whisper,
a throng's susurrus at the Mona Lisa, and she herself:

What does this moment mean, of death towarding, in terms of my death?
How does this position serve my proximates for so preparing?

Imagine asking that!

Do we owe this inversion of natural wonder
to the disenchantments of Nietzsche,
caught inside a mind's hall of mirrors,
and determines not only that he is determined,
but all of history, all of humanity,
all of life is determined—

What the matrix fan-bros would call a simulation.

And to gin freedom, he writes aphoristic metaphysics that
kill the angry god,
and rule his day with Apollon pursuits of the grave,
give the power of night to Bacchus,
thereby slay the dragon
and reorder the constellations as they fill his snipped sky with recoloring fire.

And when that new heaven didn't free him,
but painted further into a clown's listless and open-mouth glower,
he lit toward a blond savior

who could bust through the prison
and lead a race to green pastures, that he could claim to grandsire bulls.

But struck in an inner circling flush is N.,
so to close off and winnow the present, winnowing
his savior, his children again and again.

Until he becomes warded off on his sister,
and the rest is her will's legacy to the armbands of history.

I sat next table to Balzac recently at a jazz club.

This enormous-bellied grey grizzly
kept one eye on the stage,
but flashed to note our partnered boogie.

At the break
he ventured impression dressed as theory
(but aren't they all?)

And as he did to our swing at the music—the first he could or knew not
but no matter to him what he of music intoned,
I noted the woman seated at his side
contorting her shoulder to not slide off the chair.

And then I followed it down for why:
her under-reach kept to slide on Balzac's peripherating member—

Rodin's sculptured sketched person,
as the mistress codpieces his disquisition, emboldened and be-toned
as come squeeze-bottle blonded.

Wouldn't all theorists of dying
be instructed and beset by analogy
of the nautilus grin?

The energy of its nature s(n)ailing within,
deliberate and broaching, but sensing chi to slow
at the switchbacks and jibes,

recurrent until its bell fanfares spinnaker launched, and for
the preserve of a shell-statured silence?

To make note of moment and look for its death!

Such confirmed and finalized
by the whinnies of a horse being whipped
or taking state promotion in the party
that drilled its promise to *Zieg*-freed a march of *Sein* out of *Zeit*,
leaving *Seiende* behind?

Or rather to ungate from program to find in moment its pulse,
and sew spaghetti-straps to its angles of lure and tingle by verse
and leave such to billow, beckoning?

As a mountain lake gleaming with a surfaced dappling sunshine,
luring divers and anglers
to plumb its depths and halt its dam diversion—

And a physicist to wave her torch
into where this particle and poem decays
and by emission proxy its orbital energy higher
until collected by rainbows,

Propagating telic waves by tongue,
hope's saltlicks for seekers who open to will and come now thirsting
for such lakes and call and detox.

PSALM 2:2-3 AND THE DEEP(ENING) STATE

The political shear breakfasts to scene Belshazzar to rearward.

Canute commanding the Channel to turn back,

Xerxes whipping the Hellespont to impel its bridge.

with 300 chains.

Back, damned spot; out, damned history.

We send time backward by our command

to halt any more. Entries.

Ever we will build our powerful engines

to fiftytwo back the rolling tide, and implode emergencies,

you know we will.

Sigh. Eh.

Ah. Ohmm...

SAN FRANCISCO, SEPTEMBER 9, 2020

I. Apocalypse Harbored

Remember skyfall, that end of summer still-born dawn?
That sky—once looked to for rainbows—
cast a crucible, birdless and ominous, forged by wildfires—
carboniferous vampires—and
like before a hurricane—*flag-limp space.*

This sunset:
a prospect blanched, never greening, resonating
but faded to scorched amber.
Damp, sticky miasma smears like grease
to grass-hosted palms holding the pen
that attends this drama of dying shop
running emp(l)aced.

In ebbing ticks,
we by cloud castles of whipped sand construct
diversions for hollowed-out courage.
So *clocks, in this narcotic smokescape,*
ever fade from sense.

II. Sunfreeze

2–1/2 hours after sunrise,
a still dimming sky.

Under the cloaking soot from up north,
marine fogs may stay saddled to us,
bridling this apocalypse—

leaving us panting, as
under a statued Eos ginned by agora fire
to sickle a market will and grand its fix.

Else Shiva pipe a redoubt and rerealm us.

Yet today, the neap of steady alarm we will sleep through:
this day's dawn is its sunset frozen.

III. Rahner Whispers

Not arrow drawn by Mars' bow,
whose flight intends none but
a stranding vanity—a vacuum flute—
boxed in Zeno's canyons, unechoing and sere,
as the flooding for a moment lies buried.

But Thy Kingdom come's assertion is ripening,
we sniff for it amidst this foul condition.

IV. Eternity Now

Duty is the eternal present breathing.
Presumption must not but abide its hope.

No step-major can a global change for us prepare;
rather, now is our ear reeled
by children's lament of the marketplaces.

Our duties no longer allow eterne's neglect:
The present corners of streets and wildlands sweat,
wheezing.

LAST MONDAY

Your hip wakes docked at mine,
I oar to it, my palm at its gunwale, my ear its oak
aware of rippled breath.

More outward towards chasms, I canoe against waves
tenting your knees and staved ankles,
as *a sunflower turn salting and yellow*
lathes its guide by a petal's coursing—

Like finger tippling Your gluey eyelids, they dream through me, their
haven my coarsened hands less coarsening,
still to the deeper cays cast, a line to
the morning's understories
and the claim its berried star makes *tapping, kneading, urgent.*

Our clasp is waters' summoning g(r)asp which we bare emerge

To speckle the orisoning shelled sky, and noon the fettle of day.

A WHISPERED *CREDO*

Shattering the idols of closed systems,

The drive of poets is to locate, to struggle with the echoes of the locked heart.

Rather than an engraved image that appropriates futures,

Beauty erupts by vector, a power for life sprouting unending.

Stone mirrors intent for order by grey torpors; living grace mirrors life bringing.

Imagination, Spirit-watered, is its grammar:

The Embodied moment reaches toward—even pierces—the Logos

to grasp the New Adam Prometheus unbinding,

as poet prisms his throw at shadow's vanquish.

Christ bridges not heavenward to repose, but earthward arches back

to the sources and springs of eternal life brought and found.

Christ not merely the revealed center unchaining

but conduits our become

perfecting pens and trowels, extending centers but as only oases for others' minds, where compassion washes the ground of understanding.

Divine energy limbos through the gaps of despair, such we found;

Entropy balks at endings—that too we found; But grace sings of beginnings,

Wiping the residue of cogito-as-religio,

the inexhaustible fountains grace over despair

to douse its false, tethering flame

to moths worming anxiety and estranging.

Dissonance seeds its mother, its divine harmony no statue knife-shapen, declaimed; but

Look: Logos invites, not orders or chains.

Every gesture toward grace reframes mortality, destinies,

torching a light from Christ rightly sensed brings us,

The smile that endures by the heart's created intent, as

third heaven bridges its spark through our (h)earthen heart's journeying.

Always by the exhausted speaks through

Day's third dawn, fiddleheads

Fuguing about, uncoiling

Cables and rockribbing, zippering

Molten chasms of chaos for

Over(s-p)lays inside grace's tendrils of support.

Eternal life jerks from the detritus of mortal strifing—

A hook pruning the spear's moment,

As lays the plow to salt and secrecies.

LISTENS THE HELM, WRITES THE RUDDER

In the Brown(ian) cello ambient,

hydroglyphs of dusk low

by murmurating calm sea's

Tensile flecks of spume that

wetten my cheek,

while my ears dowelled

to the vessel's prow

as it knickers and splashes its wry

glue to my joints

so I come to buck and shimmy with yaw,

and—

a covenant now,

even with the sea

written by brining hoar?

Now lands—

accountability's recovery that

broaches with valid poetry for modern's recovery,

its state-of-nature-craft—

neither an elite's alienation brining

nor saloned delicacies on the Revista couching,

but ontological survival work:

facultative,

shuttered to re-yar,

de-rooting primal brambles,

cultures of death

as recede from lectern to pit,

allowing Source to fuse and flex,

to re-enter

and propriocept ambients to pacify.

X.

Wending from Lethe to the Styx
Judgment kindles when Sensorial
Denouement is attempted

—When profiteering Artifice dressed by mystique summoned Obeisance—

chatte j'ai pété quatre- zéro

and where smolders in matted purr, putting

tokens into the machined infinite—by adumbrates, analogously.

"For those whom the gods intend to destroy, they first make ridiculous" (Psalms 115:8; 135:18).

Prophetic iconoclasm DE-LIGHTS by way of satire
and grotesquery's mirrored beginning (Isaiah 44:9–20)—then
re-members the cosmos through mourning's midrash of participatory
repair.

OF COMPACTING THE PRESENT FOR ITS TRASH ORES

A Maskil for (De-)Throning :

Wadi Wallows Masskills,

Q-afar rules—oil-smeared, emitting

directed but ghosted sets of deadening fossil profets.

Technocratic curating, Oases ru(i)ning, conspiratorially monk-etic.

Of compacting the present

    for its trash ores,

to seat and ken with the Technocart,

to throttle the moment—

    up, or is it down?—

we can't know which

until we push play,

    invoking our Palm

        as to some unknown, unowned—

That we may unbutton from account.

Barren, secreted promontories all,

and waterless moats

     coursing through the valley of Sin.

Only but bea(u)tified goats,

hewing a tumble against Mount Gilead's slopes,

to avalanche De rerum, the cud-chewing,

urethra kegeled and Yclamped,

enta/isis of Bashan's beast—

whereof Choreo-likening's comb

     parting space:

If by retribution's dreamt undrawing

is backshadow resurgent,

score settling for the resentful, negated of their due—

But all I sought was stopped clocks,

and to jumpstart there an absolute

where granite outlives documenting,

     to bring back the dawn before this day's night.

Pilgrimage from Trashtent

—prolepsis or flashback?

Born with the pilot light

    of original wink,

and drenched by diremptories, caravans,

    stub-bearing,

        over-reaching and-arching shoulders.

The mistakal moment:

Societies of decorum,

    militarist gloom dispensed by codes of hierarchy,

layers of suitcoats offering the illusion of embodied security—

    the fragrance of manors and bleach-jacketed servants—

    in the stenching air of fragmentation and desperation,

    delaying the inevitable throated,

aching sentiment elided never by consequence.

The early years of life in a cradle

    ever determine taste,

fluff and feather—kernel's cowl canapés—

    that float on in the same veins of breeze as hatched,

    a landplaced death Ori(s)on—

a kabbala of phenomena,

      deep-mining consciousness

      by drug and block to chain,

      to necktie absent intent—

a get-out-jail-free deck,

      making a denim of séance and dermis

      feinted by Templed heart's discernments.

In singularity

      read through Hawking rigor or through Musk speckules,

which has standing?—

      the volcano to demand its patterns smoke,

or the lava-flight

      to scope which pattern break?

In the pitted breaks and latter

as a stubbed toe broaching

      the shutting cattle gate,

a narrowed and crooked course, interrogating

by flaps-up tongue and current,

      to jolt mercie awake,

through intervening angel-strait

than abyss chiselings,

no matter the statues or our path,

save it vibrates and whiskers still.

At shepherding table set—then

a Prophet's Tent,

but for a King,

    contemned,

by his rival betrothed.

These seed covenant,

the descent of partnering joints.

Take the reins of this Technocart,

to throttle claims of

    capacitated sandings,

transcendents atl-atled by robot arms—

since no matter how thin your microtome slices Spinoza's toast,

    there are always two sides.

Try we Gödeling to alpine horns:

    binary baking—

      system seep and

          shrinking violets,

          violent pistilation or

hegelian egirl Sandwiching,

    stuffing unity by fulsome

        clarions self-singing.

These Lofted physiques,

    aim their trunkward liturgies

for a future physic,

    better—

if for only hope signatured and ligatured,

    only if for myself, a cognition's sinew.

SPECIOLATRY

from your oiled gaze
   I see implanted
   cortical trails of a mirrored past,
   its effete deadness—
   resurrected by superannuated binaries
   only to drag you
   into its null sets
   voided by your already, too soon carriage:

Whose is the strategy,
   ivied and green zombie?

It is the dust
   that rises to test you:

What exchange can you offer dust?

Only tears to water,
   like those plants valued, Logos
   left behind—

if truly you believed
   that clay was the raw nuptial with water,
   the self-capacitated,
   canalizing electricity
   for In The Beginning.

Tears then only—
   but can your dried ration
   of silicon's ghost
   supply any such barter

on this stardusting,
    speciated (n)ovum of planet,
    where companions
    have cried out
    their last drippings?

But like Thales now at sea—
    you are cutting dung
    from clouded time
    and calling it mystery's
    beauty and truth—

a seashar(d)ed moment
    out of this mirror-glassing beckons,
    a worm its scope,
    ands tunneling through
    deadened sense.

Who will decipher its
    scratched tablet
    that swirls underneath with fading memories' magma—
    sea shot excreted
    to wine-shadow its casting—

toward its abyssals flushing
    of what we consecrate
    by poisoning, resisting
    the infinite vector stores, its housing, sometime dancehall winds?

Or maybe a metaphor will serve,
    to conjure
    repentant moistness

you existentially demand
    at this exceedingly, very Miletan moment?

Can a metaphor summon life?
    It must—
    its tears why poetry endures—

But in this heightened Now,
   can it slake your throat
   now drawing in
   the dust of (l)ashed,
   lobbing sparks
   into a backwarded night

to flood by panspermic phoenices,
   trigeminals not binaries,
   coded someward?

HIDING EGGS THEATER

Because Mid-Modernity paws Holes,

Βλέπετε οὖν ἀκριβῶς πῶς περιπατεῖτε (Eph. 5:15).

For the runny-nosed pup with invidious claims,
    snuffles for a master *taxis* inside a model curtsy lure—
    where Being is mon(k)ey's hollow conceit alone:
        absolutized,
        canonized,
        idolized,

and reducing like acid sulfur.

For the individual that is a radical isolate,
    alienate from heartmaking and keeping
    by shrunken froms—
        severed from spirit

    thru Philistine columns simplified,

  rowed for profiteering:

a jawbone's uncompromising banshee,

  cross-summons bonds of ancestral dreaming.

"Let the dead bury the dead,"

  as so Jesus said it,

Away from me all systemizers and suffusers.

Ours entombing past guns

our awareness of stun—

  in silent sun a sneer detected runs:

Dracula's—logician, dotard,

  twin fangs ramifying, exsanguinating by

  opposed categgoricals

    toward small cracked (h)ends;

Frankenstein too—knifed taxidermies,

  identity-making, ripping living wholes,

  jamming together mix-matched treads

    for fanged cats, partisan monsters, pharaoh's purr.

And don't ignore the zombies—

    lurching the lambent by resentment's frieze,

    drool scoping vengeance, open mouth, closed lung to the ambient and warm.

I'm rused to youstirring,

A ro(o/a)stery never arriving,

A wry, balled irae, chroma

Instead by stream-filtering liquored peers, the leafy run-off ink

Of hills northern spying

At our diseurs and diseuses

To propose and index is to reveal

a code for civilization

solsticeries:

The Alt-acad Rootstocks,

    bent and half-lidded ecstasies of Dennetted, untenting oases,

    climinal pottery—

such verse dashed against cisterns and walls

    to waken past the necessary dawn,

its White-Jacketed Orders,

Societies of decorum—militarist gloom

dispensed in codified hierarchy,

layers lacquered to feign embodied security—

the fragrance of manors,

and servers in bleached constraint—

all at the price of

aching sentiment elided

by irreality's consequence.

Cradled early, taste is carved—

fluff and feather, kernel's cowl,

canapés of brass drifting in the breeze

that bore the hatch and horn.

Thus we slid—

from playground's bluff

to the lifelong dark night

of the machine-making twitch,

repudiating every *telos*

with a smile glazed in ceremony:

a Tommed Holiday

    under googly eyes' dysvision,

its experience of simulation

    is mirroring dyscognition,

        absent coherence

save radical detachment from what is hidden in plain sight—

    whence one is given

        into the shadow singularity

            of ravening machination,

                striving for its remnant and determining recollect.

So throats its Coriolis wattle-twist to port,

and for a Goebbelled, gobbled möbius

    goblined by star board-ed

        axonal, vatic reverie?

I chant this loud for you, God,

    that it pierce the strangle

    and modes of synthetic venom that squelch

By Bible and cartridge

    and cross-necklaced spouse up front—

mortality sardonicus,

breath of brown,

    a bow scraped turtled cello,

    seeking a Gulf coasted advantage, wheezing

until heart-vanged by gravity

    into service-berthing a haven-hand,

    to stacking kindling

    from pyric absolutizers

And blazon vectors,

shifting seasons

    and vers-ed fawnings

and come as re(c)lines

    of pastelated dusk.

THE ARMCHAIR BECKONS (PSALM 7:15)

Speculators are weaklings—
    either through nature or through practice.
If nature gave them weak organs, weak irritations—
    as all weakness tends toward subtlety—
they were thereby determined
    to serve holy abstraction.
—Herder

Its Frankenstein impulse to be served:
"*Or they mutilated themselves,*
through abstraction weakening sensation,
until they became incapable of whole sensation . . .
In both cases, one is dealing with the sick."

First, their abstractions nest doubt in your consciousness.
Self-mutilating abstractions
    deny your sensations,
    displace your accountability

And make you doubt your awareness.
This epistemological softness is loopy—
    its chiaroscuro of probabilism and hedging,
    its conversational artifice—
is now the making of statues.

First they discourage you,
    calling you cowards or traitors—inner ring fallouts.
Then they sabotage you
    by their academies and robed honors.
Then they diagnose you
    by their white-coated hobnobbed thinkery manuals.

Then they placate you
>	with a job offer *(see Biberkopf, Franz).*
Then they come for you—but cannot find.
>	They have fallen and cannot get up.

For these abstractors of
>	mutilate perception
>	by whirlpools of self-engaging notions,
twitching tautegoricals of anatomy-fixation—
>	grey canvas shades,
>	a selfie-mirrored descent
into agency-robbing debility,
>	ignorant of pasts
>	and groomed by feedback from a larcenied future.

One is here dealing with the abyss.

ATTENDINGS

Frivolous featherweights of the pleasant
    and posed of a beautiful possess:
asides like twee coughs, coiffed nosegays,
     witticism dressed as aphorism,
belletrists and beaux artistes,
    poet physicians seeking wasted acclaim,

      fiddles unstrung in the mind's carburato-ration,
        newspapering crinkling by soot and smoke,

     blinding us by dark bits.

Aesthetic disgust solo forces them to redoubt
    with circus wagons of ancients
      before cancer's eruption,
by description alone, absent ethics,
    as if the latter birthed the diseasings;
grocery list accounts gussied in verse
    where one never departs constraints of naturalism
    nor awakens to metaphysic—
that what draws is less faith's demand
    than the rouge of lipped sacred stylizing,
a braided horse tail bobbing out paradox
    clutching the romantic late barnstorming.

Lawyer-investors in cinema projects,
painter-philosophers, versifying historians,
hypothesizing surveyors and well-grubbers
    diverted toward planting onions,
      than a wined better dousing to their unease and anxiety.

All these neglect unrelenting investigation
     uncovered in fierce and serrating syntax,
encompassing hallucinatory visions of the terrible
     and disorienting years of the middle modern age
that wanders through Christ-making ends, but
comes for lifelong dark night
     of the machine-making nest.

A garden's riot color amidst its untending,
a mangy ear pretending,
freshets a maelstrom fronting,
and a clarion, too, sounding:

Prophecy:
for one prone to ratio,
by ratio one comes prone.
(Psalm 115:8; Psalm 135:18; Luke 6:38)

So say you then, can these verses
by bootstrap you ascend?
Or the anisogamic grasp where flattens

both soil where you adhere and ideas which you align:

Can you believe it?
Can you believe that all (pros)theses work for the good?
That self-elected ontogeny
is your garden coital bed devoid of its thing—

Gimlet-eyed you come, I might have said,
but now shape-shifting your pupils for
the binar-eyed project—

come so by the phenology of weeds so of weeding

Or by its absent pistil that's curio seeding?

Either, I blow back any suppurates whence they come;

    Fallen now, yellow-eyed ratio, we

       dart an interrogating tongue with nothing of yours but to fail.

We under the shadow of Judgment Day yet attend

As another garden sussurates and becomes.

WOUNDS ARE A SIGNAL OF THE VANITY OF VIOLENCE (JOHN 20:27)

    The subdeployed macho, submachined bearer,

        the flag jingo,

            the celebratories

                belching combustion of data

                    drive-by performance of disorder,

              the in(i)quirkdity

                  of Reichstag fire space launcheries.

Far from the Madding Crowd's "Blind by self-beguilement,"
Nemo, Solo(n), ante mortem beatus.

Yet such woundings are mirrored, so too their healing:
The showcase of God's power is not heaven lighting
    but providence grounding,
        not appropriation but arrival.
The vast love on display—

    resourced for Providence—

        centered not in Mind,

            but in the One,

The aligned heart

    for what has

        and continues to unify.

The obligation

    for the celestial estate

        of children onward coming?

Awesome in grounding,

    and justice-scoped soul.

If by retribution's dreamt undrawing
is backshadow resurgent,
score settling for the resentful, negated of their expect—

But all I sought was stopped clocks,
and to jumpstart here an absolute
where granite outlives now-documenting,
    and bring back the dawn before this moment's night.

In singularity
    read through Hawking rigor or Musk speckle,
which has standing?—
    the volcano to demand its patterns smoke,
or the lava-flight
    to scope which pattern break?

In the latter valleys:

as a stubbed toe broaching
    the shutting cattle gate,
a narrowed and crooked course, interrogating.

by whiskering electrics,
    to jolt and awaken mercie,
by intervening angel-strait
    than abyss chiselings,
no matter the statues or our path,

save it vibrates mercie's full quiver still.

CHRIST'S SUBORNING ESOTERIC—

    like Spanish moss dripping
        and twinned by lichen leaf, rare patination to burnished oak leaves,
pastelated flake filigree by clouded forestations—

Needles by exoterics' valor
        that squelch the heart's unbinding.
Un-facile-making-to-order syntheses,
        fraying robed embassies
until the patron suckle of razor Rome,
        tunneling fo(u)rth, is exposed by its pelt-ings.

Corrupt forms cherished in synesthetic assembly—pushed,
        ungating to abrade arriving possibles,
in abundance characterized—
        so too of these metaphors—
essentialize all of *nature* not by romance
        bearing contingent transcendence we salute,
but as a glimpse of swaddling, honored energy by suggestion:

its hinting not to phenologies' kabbalist analogue,
        or primitivism by the submystical *valid* and da-aware—
the escape to ever deeper or farther
        oases subterranean—
but to kaleidoscope wave and nave
        that table with the luminescent over-stretching bid and palm
amidst the flyboy stock and floatline brigands

    quartered, ever destined to contrapasso
    or deriveted by purgatorial dreamworks.

Poetry douses
unentitled culture mess into afterphysics:
    careering thermodynamic laws
        and conative resystem by system opposing—
to point at what is ceaseless by the lightening and vivid;

its genius is to control fury at taxonomy,
    its directing movements of favor by wink's gestation,
        instead by irony and mashup,
the hegemonic falsities
    ever necromantic,
fragmenting shards of robbery's stone,
    that dam(n) and stifle e(nli)venings,

baptismal flows of birthings grace.

At Goethe's proper height—
not apices material
but from the reflective, recollecting, past-surveying
    of promontory trained,
tethered and jibbed to Rorschaching cloud,
the wise stakes to time and space—

For an earth-shining poem of a Christ-shown earth—
    that breathe muscle into dancers and children.

THE EAST HILLS EMERGE

under third heaven by

        chiaroscuro, shelling greys,

    where salmon come soon to run and scale shellac

        as dawn's flaxen wakes,

    umber suffusing to tawny peach,

   a chromatic course contoured by yellowing,

      firmaments washing, wiping

    through the sun's canon and brining eye

   aim to my pillowards idyll planning to rouse,

limb pulse on the rocks, liminal, hills' waking,

chill and stilled,

no chaser, no rod.

A GREAT LAKES' THEODICY

The lover hers never bested,

    mystiqued to shadowscape me, g(l)oating torment.

Mystery of mastery became

Mistakery, her echt skid:

    Dave from Grand Haven—better should from

Piscataway, and Edmond, an unCount-ed Fitzg.—

Lud's last hip wrecked on a beer-surf inland drunk,

    Hewn-Ron sinking anchored iron-eyes

        downward to skud Chebar turquoise

upward from outscaping rust, launched into the abutting

    eros-erosive airs up long Mackinacked way;

Naw: thereway—theirs, a Möbius ever there-ing,

Screw you, Waylon, we're dancing.

But me: Attendant, changing shoulders.

    Ever horizoned slipping by sacred,

Though she sits just across a table,

abluting the inscaping hard nightly settle,

backwashing the Eeries.

HEAVEN'S SEVENTH, WALKING

*Sweat*iness walked into a room—and I found effort *sweet*, corn's popping.

*Wit*ness walked—and I found its thresh *wheat*, futuring.

*Weak*ness—there was a latent *wick*, bound to oak another flame.

*Heart*less? It was only rooming *head*ness, d(r)ying.

Tears-fulness came last, expunging *tares* of the past.

And *Blood*less? *Selah*.

Washed to string slung by walked swashes.

ANENDOPHASIAC

Signed, sealed, and signifired,

Yo-hand, Georg Meetengreet Ham-mann.

"Remember that between a third and a half of people
have NO inner monologue or dialogue.
They don't debate with themselves,
they have no inner conversations—
they exist in a blur of images and sensations and feelings"...
means up to 72.37% of people don't have a talk-talk talkative brain

—like animals, soulless?
Would the Cappadocian Basil brother assent?
Have they entered into the valid testing realms
on the Stygian way, to developing essence and potential?

An inner monologue that won't STFU,
so I have to put a poetic bullet—
quicker than meds and meditation—
between its ears
and move into an undiscovered country
bordered by seas of irony
and armies of cynicisians.

Akin to the way ancient poets would write
with no sight a brain,
but with a mythic cosmos
of andro-psychic deities transmogrified by fable.

A sentience about phenomena,
separating from nature

by armchair metaphysicians,
one negating all heart through absolute freedom—

and oh boy,
those who negate freedom by having "internal dialogues?"
The lightbulbs are listening!
And the earworms of meme and irony
isn't literary convention
but muses Norma, Liza, and Prudy,

Broadway of silicon sisterhoods determining fate!

Isn't dialogue prima facie insanity,
a mental intricating standoff of limbic and logic
that hints at a park bench in the hails of spew, the seating metes topping
mother superior slush, musing mute avatars—
consistent with Leibniz's spying possibles—
or a stage of thought's fugue
toward embodying with the divine heart,
where the inner dialogue
comes to heart guide through solvings?

Nah, just introverting.
And the 72.3 mas o menos%?
A different harbor and quantity, 10:27 of John. Is this:

"I think you know. . . but they can't."?

Or Herr K., and Doktorkindred N., H., and Br., maybe, just maybe
there are multiple allowances for pathward thinking—
upstream of conscious
by a chatty womb for product dev. . .and prior to John,

or parted prior to system awaiting:

Voice: "Buck, what'ya think?"
Owens: "These ditties write themselves."
Another voice (me?): "No they don't."

UNDER SECOND HEAVEN: A THEODICY OF ARREST

Walk me through your morning dew—
Ambush trappers, predators—
    thou Manti(d)corps—

Eco's roseate brother am I,
    Salvatore,
Experi-pla(n)ting words
    of geld and gelding,
        not lib/terate,

But a philology
    for the sake of an armchair con,
coining the hearer
    into theaters of entropy's
        sand moats and closure—
with no saving curtain save cloud
    pregnant with duststorm
        and light(e)ning.

(To speak, Salvatore,
*   *rather than just read**
*   *as does the abbot—**
*   *I hear he's writing**
        The Beauty of the Ergodic—
in a foreign language
to shrink from
*   *of its lifeless courtier sulcus.)**

And then the defense rises:
Our tractors lack free will
    because we do,
And thus we are gelded
    by determination's original seeds of sin.

Physicians can't heal themselves,
    take a decision—
Can they?
    No geld in it.

QED:
    "Not guilty"?

SANDTRAPPED BY THE MARS INVITATIONAL

Destiny's not going to go well for the boosters:

the claim of "inevitability"

    reveals both Husk and Huckster.

A claim that satraps

    trusted determinism,

and the hegemonic ken

    of its hallucinatings and ketamining

        are evidence of caddies tonturing

the airless, brown scudding army noon for The Green Jacketed.

Are you struggling with your golf swing?

I guarantee, more than the old college try—there's a wrist implant for that,

a pith, a *lobot,* Helmut,

bluetoothed to your meme-and-surveillance-addled cortex.

Therefrom, the heartbreak of bogies shall be no more.

Come, let us reason:

by turns meting, addle-leaf blowing,

and efficiently calibrated by psoriatic passions.

The very agency of *play-ins*
    toward a machined self
        gives it standing
in forensic investigation—challenge.

But to maintain and grow
    a just society
        within a criminal irreality—
a pithed culture,
    simulacra pithing simulacra?

Speaking paradox here, a training by recurrence and stymie,

not a deep cushioning mystique,

A dog eating grass—
    or is it the worm in its gut
        re-dirt wombing,
as a ball's dimples
    rigorously assemble
        to code its claim,
            coursing toward its singular, determining hole—

        emptied of covenant, its whiskering ear?

Justification by what piths

    is the appropriation of belief

        by the path of attribution

with what one will align.

Not a helmet,

    but a *spining* needle

        followed by...

what alienates from the one

    where the other claims

        a mind divorced

from the one

    but...

Such efficient and physicalist "brain science" of member-guest

    leads to corner-cutting, finance,

        cost-bunkering.

The illusory epiphenomena

    of a fundamentally mindless,

        aimless,

            unthinking virtuality

                of material ends

are grounded in no prior

    transcendent,

        or relational absolute.

Where civilizations

    of thin and ends-directed cognition

        is certain to collapse into terraforming putts,

tricks of synthetic greens clipped and sand's sold(i)erings:

Data and Orion's design

      that sever the spirit of humanity from God

          and ginned toward evil sleepings—

Surely nothing

    can come from that

      but the severity

of a locked abyss

Zippering the day's muscle-memory,

bounding *Prepostero's* s(l/w)inging seed with a round

of time and accountability

all for the sake of your drive.

LUDD'S LAST STAND

God as light wave

    coincidences the eternal

        in back and forth movement—

    of approach

        and retest's withdrawing.

And as particle to send us on our way:

    the sabbath welcome

        and comfort already realized.

I feel a deep sabbath sadness

    for every student lost to AI—

        in an essay,

            or a lover's missive,

                or any neighbor

    who mines AI to shaft

        letters of political ardency

        and commitment.

For they become ensorcelled,

    chained to hoist shadow vomits

    thrown from the past, till now not catchered,

    that only hoped, at best,

        for the most minuted recurrence—

though such a particle

    drops not from a circle

        but from wave's propagate direct.

So no rainbow of release

    may appear.

Nature's Meataphysics are

    Mete-aphysics of Muskifying genera,

    crypto-Ration and austere-making

    for the aggrandizements of vestment(alent)ed

        wannabes and goons.

So Lud's Last stand wars upon

    whether tech-capitalist patriotism

        or state-designed

    for a humanity

        of gargantuan infomatics.

Hamlet: the time is out of joint / o cursed spite! / that ever I was born to set it right.

Fated—

    but you go through it

To new pasturing.

Nesting Space, Unreserved for Dr. Lidd

I had seen the sign:
    Space Reserved for Dr. Lidd.
I'd come to lathe an identity
    from condition. Heid-aggue's last placing lane, a shut-eyed afterimage,

a '90s freeway without offramp: the *Brain Diabetic*.

He explored my black box
    from the saddle,
whips and scalp(el)s
    training my desire
for his black bag job
    of cultural sagacities—
therapeutic raconteur therapy,
    pills from apithi-caries radical and unknown,
an occasional hit of keto,
    and sequestration privileges
at the local lockbox—
    where he has another reserved space
for his ride.

Rara avis, Dr. Lidd, his screen tells him, but cannot answer:
What kind of name is that?

Yet I know he was born that sat on an egg,
    Herr Doktorvater Mutmacher,
but he's tanned now, like the wheat-ripe stars
    suite-d to sweeten the brow of its hills.

He can fold you into the DSM,
    or make the DSM
        do the same
into you.

He's Dr. Lidd,
    OBE, VV, Psy.D., MBA (Accounting).

By his tricks—
    ahem, interventions—
He hoofs me into
    the Pithicanthropocene implant,

Reserved for Dr. So and So.

Say goodbye
    to all that.

Soon he'll be parking
    in the distant psychotone—his own nipped wing
between painted lines
    and axle-wrecking curbs,
        waddling it in like the rest of us.

Not because the revolution holds,
    but because
the miasma of therapists
    have cleared the lines.

Him not least.

No longer Post hoc,
    propter Doc normalcies—
irrigator of soul ecologies
    by calibrated, speciated mechanics,

his specula through spectrums,
    spectral prismatic flagworks
of nip and tucked gonadal corticals
    here and there.

I hear he will be writing poetry of billing codes' unmooring

"The Intensities of the Quod Ergodic."

Critics will crow and chime and which I am booted—

this rara Avis rental nestednessing, post-docked.

A-NULLING (A CODA)

The liar-influencers' redoubt—

    intelligencing's inexorables

    couched in operational impersonating implodes of mysticism—

Shiva who jigs another world for those who bow to it—

is already run off from its bluff.

You see it suspended midair,

    like Wile E. Coyote:

its impos(T)ers contemplating their state of nature

    with just enough slacked grace

    to either repent

    or collapse.

Or in the closing image of The Great Gatsby:

    the 53-joker system deckhands,

    yawled by Pneuma not to their intended course,

    but, in an iron-clad reversal,

    to the sand-loins of its sewers—

    the eternal return of its pulled pasts, yanking back—

the tug of war always roped by dirempted pull of the null set

Where looms

    a swirling

    and (com)pressing nemesis:

Not a landfall's brilliance of mind

    but arrogance's Nightfalling,

        where a circuiting brain aggrandizing by tricks

grows ever more dim.

Go tell Uncle Tom Giddings the Miner:

Manners' purified sense are still entropies never riser can from dust whence light put them for roses' flickered delighting.

POSTLUDIC

If a journey in Christ comes
via the philosopher's snifter and cushion—
not by jowl-moistening repentance—
it arrives by endorsement of another sublime,
the inner ring magnet of escape from awe,
from accountability to justice flying by
the false flag of freedom—
self-determined,
self-tethered—
and thus to sink against the copse of coups,
grasping by sunk tendrils at whatever is held as solid,
so then lapsing, freighted by conceited
pasts buoying that come to icon riprap and
knuckle being into determined futures
where ever again security
leans by
with neither ecstasy
nor experiment gestured
nor stooping
nor becoming.

Iconoclasm punctuates
dead skins of bumptious primations (Hebrews 6:6),
humbly forthing
virtue's habituations
so the Trinitarian heart
comes to scrub history's rudder, not with sand's keel abrading,

but the soap of repenting,

Torqued through nuptial liturgies of double helix—
its aureole clued, zippering, acrostically settling
human potential
and divine logos—
that cohere, concurrently,
coursing by archive's coffer
and shared cozening.

By the creature's bearings
eternity's shed seed,
by sense made dendritic,
a waterbug poised to
the water surface
of embodied generations—
hosting arriving rivers of possibles
of sailing grace,
rather than damming off or self-sheeting

to evolve reformed or deformed triangulates
of jawbone and canvas
against the masted horizon—
a hierarchophaging spinnaking—
(b)luffing and breeching
toward statue'd heavens
as haven
from history's broaching.

FRAGMENTS AND FOUNDLINGS

A coda or marginalia by shards of metaphysics. These revolt from absolutes detached from the body—a withdrawal that serrates the heart's syntax. Yearning both A Priori and Absolute is the ontology of our Becoming yet may be at our ends stranding–a storm shoring of Proverb.

"The heart set on stone canonizes transactional altars."

"Maps of historical recurrence destroy human potential invisible to professor and priest."

"More should meteorology than cartography a poem."

"Poetry channels divine energy into emerging cultural archives."

"Against the type and temple dead weights progress trains its light."

"Poetry joins—indeed leads—modernity's reluctance to enter priesthoods of human grasp whence accountability vitiates."

"The Attribute negates the Appropriating."

"Beware: Finitude cannot contain grace's infinite possibilities."

"Wrath comes grammatical, mercy a sermon from sustaining proprioceptive chi

Like massage or sandwich made by another's bettering hand."

"Eternal time stoops."

"Language unbankrupts when freed from debt-chaining authority of forms."

"To shell with eternity comes forlain with weight and rigidities atop one's soul, but to crack its gate is to soar by language nonetheless."

"Hope divorces from irony's effete perch."

"To rise up from civilization is to be bested daily by tests between fining and declining, of nemesis and eros."

"Sin chains time for the sake of position, repentance unbinds and re-launches both."

"The heart is the embassy of open eternity to enclosures of philosopher and monk."

"Form closes by chisel what grace, geology's waters to stone repurposes."

"Entropy ever gestures for endings; righteousness is grace's filibuster of renewal."

"Each failure alive is sewn with seeds of eternity."

"Consider the seasoning for human essence, how we blossom swaddled by divine energy, for that history demands hospitalities."

"History is composed in the emergent, rather than defined by normal, by the peacemaker than the general. All other historicisms are false."

"The Spirit waters the seeds of dormant imagination."

"A neologism is a wormed barb jigged by an unknown wrist. The bait is either taken off the hook, ignored, or is lipped and enfleshed to drag somewhere else."

"Creation's energies are never exhausted, only untapped."

"Providence is the choreography of grace."

"Heaven's angels sing of Earth celebrating the unique in us all—In a cosmic entirety, I now angel potential arrived, destined to lassoing the most meager of a fifth parting, and yet such so grand to free!"

Not abandoned to the elements—fragments are the elemental. In them speaks the necessary unsystematic, the unprogrammed, the unfinished: grace's fidelity to the imaging eternal body and heart by fibers. Not rhythm's ends but echoes and icicles—the fertile isolates of the Logos that remain when all worldly cartographies collapse under their spew, and only weathers of grace still sound.

Afterward
(Postlude as Prologue)

The parts of this anthology have not merely intended a sequence of lyric meditations but a progressive poetic theology—a metaphysical journey into vectors (more meteorology than cartography) of witness, reckoning, and regenerative craft. From conception to an era's death cradle, instruction to disillusionment, to retraining in the kinesthetic poiesis of Christ, each part is meant to deepen, fracture, or counterpose the last. The poiesis of spiritual awareness spirals from inward to outward, from lament to re-imagining, from historicism to poetic *telos*: from erosion of natural personhood of grasping to the sparked human essence called down from transcendental heights of conceit and ratiocination instead to serve immanence of the whole.

Catches by inner eyelids orange between shades of

Antic fret and gambol,

heat-coiled earthworms the color of citrus and stonefruit rotting:

rejected Traditional Pieties, or
attempts to wrest reality
by Technological Acceleration
straining to (bull and horse) shit out
evolutionary redesign
for its ape pharaohs.

Transhumans hug themselves in foxholes,
detached by loathing, irony's effete, and crawled nostalgic yearning
as under a drone-bearing sun,

a sizzling cauldron of judgment
casting its forebode pall
to arrive fierce
upon ovoid smog, horneting.

To emerge from these pocks, brambles, and boils, we come to participate in the proprioceptive, kinesthetic, and recollecting Logos unfolding from brokenness to delight, from compost to cosmos, from wound to wound-bearing witness To mature beyond a nature ligatured by archive and hierarchy, so as to realize the potential of a human essence, attuned to immanence as the Vatic Coriolis of repairing. An essence that scales enclosures by refusing to close, and instead compose and craft assayed worlds of betweenness and middle-making where entanglement with the old epoch brings undergrowths of insight into the redemptive, where grace is virtuously aligned rather than dogmatically imposed. And Satan can never escape his abyss, no matter what monkey-coded artifice is brought to bear.

Do we ask of poetic awareness as of cognition: is such a fundamental trait of the universe? Or must truth about reality be stated as a principle or ground cordoning off human possibles? Or is sensory poiesis only provisional? Is authentic understanding deterministic and causal, or probabilistic and correlational? The usual binaries mislead. Poiesis, rather, is marked by resonance and resistance in facing the immanence of conative acts. Cognition severed from conation, through categorical logic, attempts to elide accountable living—and in doing so, by its axiomatic winnowing, kills.

What is needed is a retrained modernity—a renaissance modern. Modernity began well: shifting from the institutioned proclamation of truth to the individual's responsibility to investigate and align with it. From static form and hierarchy to dynamic vector and equality of created potential, modernity turned toward history's energy of peacemaking, not the exhausted boundaries drawn by epaulooned generals. Both institution and individual once understood that accountability flows from the act of seeking human potentiality not following forms of putative human nature.

But Enlightenment individualism veered off course. Rather than pursuing a keening metaphysics, it collapsed into a radically subjective freedom-claim, forged under Napoleonic distress: I. Kant do anything without an umbrella service of subordinates—so only my thoughts may fly free, and even they must ground themselves in self-determined goals absent my created potentials! In such formulations, freedom was unmoored from metaphysics of relationship to announce a system of particular, static interiority disguised as universal absolutes.

Methodologically, poiesis centers on the virtue of recollection—not as an intuitive measure of memory, but as an ongoing investigation conducted through auscultation and archival ligature with the world in which one is contextualized and set, not randomly thrown. It does not seek forms to which an ontological and binding affinity is claimed—forms that always drag the soul backward in time. Rather, recollective poiesis involves the soul's auscultation of ontological vectors in motion, trajectories to which the soul holds affinity—whether trending toward *agon* or *shalom*: toward an eschatology of catastrophe, as is the case with all claimed, entropic formalisms, or rupture by which what is desired is re-aligned and extended but not finally overthrown because it is of the light.

Poetic perception involves punching apertures through surfaces of energy's scour and thermodynamic degradations: the intuitive serves the pre-reflective ground where divine revelation emerges, not yet philosophical or doctrinal, but moral and felt as such. Thus the poet is prophetic, who senses before she speaks, and may only be—necessarily be—prophetic because they have an ethical confidence that what they sense and perceive is the essence or its anti-essence. The poet is not merely receptive, he is developing faculties of aware attunement with the Unseen Metaphysic by means of reflective consideration of how the moral and the phenomenological align in his own purifying heartwork ("senses (*aistheteria*) trained" (Heb 5:14). What is observed changes the observer, and what light is cast onto an object changes the object. Contrary to Heidegger's valorized verse (s)training by darkness, this can be the only valid method of poiesis.

In abandoning metaphysics outside the self—precisely because of the accountabilities it entails—modernity reduced itself to a null metaphysics of worldly ego measuring. Like in the Biblical age of the Judges, each pursued what was right in one's own eyes, yet lacked the capacity to realize it. Complex chains of cause-and-effect quickly overwhelmed intention. What followed was failure, disorientation, and the ironical sense of living within the unintended consequences of one's favored stratagems and valorized orders.

A modern renaissance of accountable and virtuous poiesis is pursued idiolectically, *sui generis*—as that resists the permanence structures typical of aesthetic metaphysics grounded in anything but the heart. Say, as for Balthasar, Desmond, and Hart, in "infinite" beauty that dulls by sentiment and is given too easily to nihilism from fatalism. A theo-aesthetic iconoclasm abandons tradents that chain history to natural hierarchies and stifle human potential, instead prophetically to lance them. Poetic visceral testimony rejects harmonizing with material analogies and their categorical, cognitive syntheses. Resisting the lure of modes and models of ascendence along fixed ladders and determined patterns as rites of "participation."

Poetic iconoclasm is idiolectic witness refusing inherited coordinates while seeking new grammars of covenant, immanence, and conative effect. Poiesis reveals volatility of flame, its sourcing applied to environment: it fuses domains—in the wake of critiques of metaphysics but refusing its anthropocentric closures, established by ecological lament and Trinitarian yearning—into a mode unrecognizable to adumbrative techniques of conventional genealogical anachronisms imported to the heart absent context. Poeisis illuminates the heart in history, the heart of history, and the heart situated in environmental settings contemplating the heart (Logos) of other species and other eras. Its poetics rupture and lance in order to drain and repair—more Ezekiel and Basil the Great than Origen, more understandable Pentecostal utterance than Thomist catechism.

So poiesie may also preach:

The "thou shalt nots" do not rest easily in such a the post-metaphysical claims of the absolutized self, but the "thou shalts"—the positive imperatives—have been too easily subsumed into a freedom from metaphysics that makes the Golden Rule a *guideline*, subject to rationing among subjective ends. Of geometries of dispense that weighed lesser evils to make room for personal and strategic ends. *Ratio* as *cogito*. *Ratio* as *religio*. *Ir-ratio-guard-less*.

So modern rationality has become its own source of crisis. It embodies resource and de-creational shortages by naturalizing human myopia and greed. This *creates an a priori* rationale for ratiocination. The metacrisis of weighing ends for lesser evils, in order to exert our will tethered only to self-asserting ends.

Meta-crisis has staked humanity to "post-"s, where skeptics battle yearning and the coherence of ethics that sustain and so discard generative sight lines. Categorical logic begins with blind foundational claims about human nature, and every political statecraft begins from such a claim. Thus a poet is bound to investigate nature, and naturalizing claims about human nature. But while a state begins with "*Because* resources are limited for the public good," only the poet, Yahwist, Malthus, and Marx begin with "*Why* are resources limited for the good?" One doesn't need to be a poet to know that ratiocination proportions and appropriates public goods to the benefit of the system center, to the detriment of the marginal and periphery.

The poet, then, is ever the interrogator of statecraft, especially by a strong man ruler, of Platonic formalizing and taxonomy, and of categorical closure and categorizing logic of ration. Of ratio. Of ratiocination. Of idiosyncrasies of rationalism as natural reason. The poet offers another form of reason than ration-ism. The poet lives as nature Attributes and lists the divine as his friend and comfort, never inside the sword-bearing angels of Appropriative reason-as-rationality.

Ratio is the snake in the garden tempting in its promise to un-mete the heart from accountability to the Creator of reason, to allocate a de-creating form of reason by the freedom to determine ends, bringing nihilism upon others by rationalism's extinguishing antitheses and Boolean logics—as one freed from his garden host and mates. The whole heart for the total creation was lost, and so here we are, at the point of fractionate realities, being staked to post-s by the dragon.

To ends incapable of arriving because divorced from metaphysics, only a Titan, a Prometheus, can like a birdbath tip heaven to release us from this impasse: What can be known about the essence of the creator regarding human deathlessness for us to pursue by other means than those endowing the present crises.

Yet this heaven has already rained: the only Attribute of the divine knowable is through the son: his Sermon-mounted clarion to dispense with Appropriation, his sacrificial supplication making known the radical love that the creator has for the creation. The only humanly-knowable divine attribute is intent to sustain and flourish—the conation of heart—for endurance. For the human to arrive at her potential is to align with that heart, without ratio-ing its ends. To heart-commit wholly to the creation represented by the other, without mete or ration.

Accountability to the creator's heart for the creation is our obligation to the creation—to study and serve it as we are constituted by embodied soul. Poiesis is the method, for Adam dust-aware of the renewing essence of earth reality. What we owe:

To our lords and superiors: un-ration-ed honesty;

To our subordinates and wage earners: un-ratio-ed mercy;

To our peers: un-ration-able virtue;

To our works and callings: whole body-and-soul devotion to duty.

To those in deprivation at our footstep: unrationed care.

Religio and *poiesia* are never cisterned as limited resources, so not by ratio come.

SO UP FROM STREETSETTING GLOSSOLALIA

its Azusa flut-t-terings
charismaticians unrooting jazz on its sun-knocking
graft that claw and cloy re-madding doggerel—
might instead come Pentecost again in these,
verse thudded and wonder jolting,
willed intelligible by the main its legs and ankles,
into whence partners the room- and tent-making heart
by clutching prophecy through partnering rhythm from awareness,
cohering Logos by choresis:
And bring Paul's fourteenth chapter finish to the Corinthian
lip by othering's interpret and backleading kiss?
So that kine-thetic verse is every Pentecost's arriving speech,
striating and stretching the messianic freshets in our throating
we hope and sense.

Must so then humanity ever sealeg wing and open,

to muffling lament by a daimon,

gimlet-eyed crucible, battened and beating against

wet-wrenching ropes and rubbed camel knots

tuning the masted pass

and calling sail and mane of Christ,

our poetic and kinesthetic bearing

under the gift-giving prism lofting,

downdraftward blue,

Its feather and halo

jigging, abounding the set and bounty

galley table as it prows and plows,

two-stepping with the foamy sea,

a heeling gut weather humming

from blows the helming horn

that gladdens.

A handful of the poems in this volume had early editions posted on the author's Blog, "Crying in the Wilderness of Mammon" [douglasolds.blogspot.com].

New poetry of the author's will be posted to his successor Blog, "the iconoclast's descending" [douglasblakeolds8.blogspot.com].

www.ingramcontent.com/pod-product-compliance
Lightning Source LLC
Chambersburg PA
CBHW070234230426
43664CB00014B/2298